WINSTON...

...the dog who changed my life

HILMAR KLUTE

Hubble & Hattie

For nearly eighteen years, the folk at Veloce have concentrated their publishing efforts on all-things automotive. Now, in a break with tradition, the company launches a new imprint for a new publishing genre!

The Hubble & Hattie imprint – so-called in memory of the two, dearly-loved Westies who lived with company owners Rod and Jude for over 14 years, and gave them so much love and stoical friendship – will be the home of a range of books that cover all things animal – all produced to the same high quality of content and presentation as our motoring books, and offering the same great value for money.

This is our first book under the new imprint, which will be followed by the titles shown below, with very many more fascinating and informative books to come – about dogs, cats, horses, rabbits, goats, chickens ...

For more detailed information about our forthcoming Hubble and Hattie titles, please see page 157

Translated by Anna McLuckie
Front panel illustration 'Winston,' from an original oil painting by Jacqueline Stanhope.
Jacqueline Stanhope Fine Art 2009. www.jacquelinestanhope-fineart.com

www.hubbleandhattie.com

First published in English in September 2009 by Veloce Publishing Limited, 33 Trinity Street, Dorchester DT1 1TT, England. Fax 01305 268864/e-mail info@hubbleandhattie.com/web www.hubbleandhattie.com.
ISBN: 978-1-845842-74-1 UPC: 6-36847-04274-5
Original publication ©Verlag Antje Kunstmann GmbH, Munich in 2008
Readers with ideas for books about animals, or animal-related topics, are invited to write to the editorial director of Veloce Publishing at the above address.
British Library Cataloguing in Publication Data – A catalogue record for this book is available from the British Library. Typesetting, design and page make-up all by Veloce Publishing Ltd on Apple Mac. Printed in India by Replika Press.

C ONTENTS

Before Winston 4
What's that, then?... 11
What do you think he wants? 17
He doesn't fit with my lifestyle.... 24
We really should be more deferential 30
Winston makes his entrance... 37
The person should come to the dog.. 43
A question of training – and ear care 49
Work on the dog. 55
Breeds of owner.. 61
We have to talk – about your dog 67
To hell with the experts! .,.. 75
We discover common enemies 82
Does he go in the water too?.. 91
The dog in world literature 97
I will change 105
That is his character 108
The dog's name.. 115
Alien, and yet one of us 120
Have we really done everything right?.. 127
Appendices for the discerning dog-lover 131
    Books for fans of dogs & literature... 132
    Dog manuals that really are useful.. 135
    Famous people & their dogs.. 135
    Dogs who made history 141
    Dogs in films 143
    Dogs on TV... 144
    Dogs in cartoons 147
    Quotes about dogs 150
    Five statements to reassure anxious passersby 153
    Which names suit which breed? 154
    Miscellaneous.... 154
    Author's note 155
    'Excuse my dog' notes 156

BEFORE WINSTON ...

One evening, the dog was suddenly there. It was not planned, or wanted, and I had never had a dog in my life before. I never stroked dogs, although I wasn't afraid of them: I just didn't notice them. I found dogs about as interesting as the cricket results or watching paint dry. I was never bothered by the sight of dog poo on the grass verges. It was almost as if I had a sort of dog-blindness, in the same way that some people are unable to see certain colours or distinguish between different musical notes. I knew virtually nothing about the different breeds, and I hardly ever spoke to people out walking their dog – at least not about dogs. In the place where other people have a dog, I had a blank space.

When I was a child, I was bitten by a dog – as many other children are. The dog, a scruffy old black terrier, came running down a narrow track straight towards me and sank his teeth into my calf. It wasn't a big deal; the whole thing was quite perfunctory, almost as if pre-arranged. The dog wasn't looking for a fight, he just wanted a calf to bite and he found one; any other calf would have done just as well, so it wasn't an attack on me personally. Many people who have been bitten by a dog believe that they have been deliberately selected as a victim by this specific animal, and thereby singled out by the bite as future prey for other dogs, who will then launch brutal and bloodthirsty attacks on their arms and calves. Sometimes this even proves to be true, but I'll come to those stigmatized dog victims later ...

I didn't harbour any great resentment towards the terrier back then. The matter was sorted out by a tetanus injection, a bar of Toblerone, and some consoling words from my parents. In the years that followed, presumably, the terrier managed to replace the taste of my skinny kid's calf with other tastier, chunkier legs! So I can't say that a traumatic dog-bite experience caused me to have a lifelong fear of dogs, as is the case for many other declared dog-haters. A friend once told me about his childhood experience of a vicious dog. The events he related were certainly more dangerous than my meeting with the leg-obsessed terrier, and my friend was bitten severely on the face, sustaining injuries bad enough to worry anyone, let alone a child. Ever since, the anxiety and hatred caused by this event have resulted in his strong dislike of dogs.

A few years ago it happened that we were both in Beijing and went to a restaurant

where dog meat was served, but on the quiet and only at the express wish of Western customers. On the spot, my friend absolutely insisted on ordering the dog meat. Because this meal took place in the pre-dog era of my

life, I had a relatively neutral stance to the food. When the red meat was served, it looked good, but I didn't want to try any. With ever-increasing gratification, my friend ate the little red bits of meat, still containing dog bones and, when he had finished, announced his conclusive victory over the hostile canine world. He felt that he had got his own back. His fervour, negative as it was, both astonished and disconcerted me.

My relationship to dogs, as I have mentioned, was for many years – and in this respect they were carefree years – based on the principle of complete indifference. Every now and then, I looked out of the window early on a rainy morning and felt sorry for the owners, who, hastily washed and, probably still wearing their pyjamas, were guiding the pointless smell-searching of their poodles, who were encased in pathetic little dog raincoats, although I was less interested in the dogs than the fact that adult humans allowed themselves to be compelled into this kind of uniformity. Every morning they took the same route that the dog was used to: "Take the same route every morning that the dog is used to;" this statement, made by our dog trainer, is now one of my most important maxims, because the pleasant indifference to dogs, the era of inconsiderately fast walking whilst looking straight ahead, and my cluelessness about what happens in that busy little, knee-level world, and the constraints, laws and wondrous things it involves – that's all in the past now.

These days, I can give you an off-the-cuff explanation of dog agility; I know how clicker training works and can make mention of the benefits of dog dancing without looking in the slightest bit shifty. I always carry several little black plastic bags, and take my hat off to the freshness and originality of the Munich-based Human and Dog Forum's motto "Good will moves dog muck." In my trouser pockets, I always have little multi-coloured biscuit bones, and when I go shopping I pick up repulsive rubber chickens, chewy rings and little shoes made of tanned cowhide. It's all for the dog, because, these days, I belong to the five-and-a-half million-strong community of German dog owners. I pay 75 euros a year dog tax and have extended my third-party insurance to cover 'Pet/Dog.' I spend around two thousand euros a year on veterinary expenses, boarding kennels and training lessons, and that's not even counting the cost of dry food and the *Lekkerli* treats with their strange Swiss name.

My day is timetabled so that the dog gets as much exercise and mental stimulation as possible, as well as regular opportunities to empty his bowels. I know that I shouldn't stay away from the dog for longer than five hours at a time, because the dog's body just won't tolerate that. During the lunchbreak, I leave the office with my stomach rumbling and drive home to the dog. If I want to go away, I have to organize somewhere for the dog to be looked after. Where is our minister for ensuring more dog day-care provision? How is anyone these days supposed to combine having a career and a dog? Strangely, in contrast to the issue of childcare, the answer to this problem is simple: you can take your dog everywhere with you, even to work, for example. Children have no business in the workplace, but dogs are tolerated. However, if I take my dog to the office, I can't get any work done because I am constantly preoccupied with the dog – as he is with me; when I am with the dog, he doesn't tolerate any activity that fails to place him and his interests centre stage, and so I leave him at home.

In spite of this, he is with me every minute, as I can't stop myself from imagining how he is sitting on the sofa and rearranging the cushions, or how, following a sudden flash of inspiration, he will run into the bedroom, drag the sheets off the bed and take them away because he thinks they would be better kept in the kitchen or the bathroom. Will the rug in the hallway still have fresh colours and be entirely intact when I return home, or will the dog have roughened up the fibres and rubbed the pungent extracts from his bone into the weave? Is the dog practising being calm, or is he barking as soon as someone walks

along the hallway? Is he planning any major
alterations in the apartment? When my phone
rings in the office, just for a second, I think it's
the dog calling. Sometimes it seems to me as if,
for all these years, the canine world has just been
waiting for me to pay it some attention. Because
I didn't, the canine world took a drastic step,
which meant that I didn't just get interested in
said canine world but was completely drawn into
it. Overnight, I became part of this crazy world,
in which 'stay' no longer means having friends
for an extended visit, and where the boundaries
between human and animal become so blurred
that there is doubt whether there are actually
any differences between the species. A world,
therefore, that you can leave only through death
(the death of the dog, obviously).

You would, of course, be justified in asking
– and I would probably ask myself – why
someone who is really not interested in dogs at
all can suddenly make a complete U-turn and
follow a path which smells of wet fur, echoes
with the sound of wild yapping and the shouts
of a strange name, which initially sound friendly,
then annoyed and finally desperate? With a
suddenness that makes the hairs on the back
of your neck stand up, a powerhouse of a dog
appears, running headlong, its tongue
lolling out of its mouth like an
ironic flag of friendliness, before
finding its final target with
a determined leap up to
chest-level. The target is

9

WINSTON ...

the man who had nothing to do with dogs and
who now offers a biscuit bone to the panting
animal. I am the dog's target. How did it come to
this? The truth is it was a stupid coincidence, a
little tragedy, and a small stroke of fate.

One evening the dog was suddenly there ...

WHAT'S THAT, THEN?

My wife found the dog one cold January evening in an old cemetery in Munich. She was coming back from a seminar in Hamburg and, as she walked, heard a noise that sounded like a baby's cry. Joggers were running through the cemetery as usual, bouncing along in the darkness in their red and blue tracksuits like computer-generated automatons. They all ran past the little dog, despite the fact that the animal was whining and making a constant, pointless effort to escape the small area in which it was tethered, its freedom of movement restricted by a short, red lead, which the previous owners had used to tie the animal to a small tree.

They had simply abandoned the dog, which is not just a nasty, inhumane thing to do, but also an offence for which anyone caught and convicted would receive a large fine. In what appeared to be an effort to salve their conscience, the former owners had left a few items with the dog that might be of use if it was rescued. So, around its little neck the dog had a small, white plastic bag containing basic kit – a food bowl, a bag of Eukanuba dry dog food, and a vaccination card – a collection of items that now seem to me like a sarcastic little commentary on my life as a dog-owner. The vaccination card had been stamped in the Czech Republic and certified the dog to be a perfectly healthy animal: rabies vaccination, distemper shot – the works. However, the most significant information on the document was the name of the dog: Winston. The act of cutting the red lead bound Winston to us for ever.

That evening, the temperature was really low and the dog must have been enduring this for at least an hour. The cold had caused the little dog some problems, the most obvious of which was the frostbite on his paws. Those paws ... And now we come to a description of the distinguishing characteristics of the dog's appearance: the paws were the first things I saw when my wife stood with the dog in the doorway of our apartment.

I should say that we had occasionally discussed the idea – which we liked very much – of taking a small family of cats into our home; two, maybe even three delicate, stealthy house cats, who wouldn't be any trouble and whose always sparklingly clean litter tray would be a safe haven of cleanliness and care. Yes, we'd be very pleased to have some cats, but a dog? Never! The subject had not come up often, but, when it had, we were always in complete agreement – we would never have a dog in our home.

But on this January evening, a dog came

into our house, brought there by my wife, who had wrapped it in a swimming towel, so that at first all I could see were the paws, paws which were so incredibly huge that at first I couldn't believe they belonged to any indigenous animal. Innocently I asked: "What's that, then?"

"A little dog ..." my wife pulled back the towel "... his name is Winston." At this moment I looked into Winston's eyes for the first time. The dog looked back at me with a great deal of curiosity accompanied by fear of what might happen to him next. We unwrapped the dog from the towel and put him down on the carpet, where he began to run backwards and forwards with a wild, clumsy, wriggling gait, interspersed with jumping up at us – habits which he unfortunately still has today. The dog was silent, but gave an affirmative wag of the tail as soon as he was called by his name. I don't know if he sensed the gulf of unfamiliarity between us and him, but I felt it clearly enough and looked for ways to resolve the situation quickly and as satisfactorily as possible for all concerned.

We needed the animal rescue service, even if it was getting relatively late in the evening. The animal rescue service is staffed by dedicated young people, who come out at any time of the day or night when an animal is in trouble, even when a squirrel has fallen off a branch and hasn't got the strength to get back up the tree. They come when old

cats suddenly suffer a stroke, fat dogs suffer an intestinal obstruction, and exotic ornamental birds regurgitate their food. The animal rescue service always comes out, and it would come to our home this evening and take Winston away to somewhere where he would be well looked after and provided with species-appropriate food. I suggested that I look up the phone number on the internet.

My wife countered with the suggestion that we should let the dog settle down first. This was clearly nothing to object to, as long as settling down didn't mean moving in for good, because it was obvious that we needed to get the dog out of our house. We both work, and simply didn't have the time to look after a dog: apart from that, neither of us had the slightest idea how to deal with a dog!

Then my wife said that, apart from anything else, the dog needed to see a vet first, at which point I began to get suspicious. Why did we have to take care of the dog's health needs? We rescued him – that should suffice. On the other hand, if we took Winston for a short visit to the vet, it wasn't exactly making a commitment to adopt him. It was a fact that the dog looked very underfed, and we could only assume that he was suffering serious consequences from the lack of nourishment.

When Winston stood – or, more exactly, lay – on the parquet floor of our living room for the first time, it was our first chance to study and evaluate his appearance. Winston is a tri-coloured dog with a compact, almost cat-like body shape, and bowed, bandy little legs ending in semicircular white paws, which make him look like he is wearing tennis socks. His muzzle has the shape of a short, but elegant arc with a white fleck just before the top of his nose, like a flake of snow, a caprice of nature. His ears are big and pointed and somewhat bat-like. His eyes – that sensitive realm in which it is possible to see emotion, childlike characteristics and mawkish projections – are triangular and dark brown in colour.

The surprising thing, which I also found rather perturbing, was that the dog didn't seem to be worried by the strangeness of our apartment, and behaved as though he had had a long and rather exhausting journey, encountering a number of hassles along the way, but had now finally arrived in his carefully pre-booked hotel where he could be certain of a meal and a bed for the night. We poured his Eukanuba dry food into a bowl and watched as he ate moderately and with great concentration. (I have to confess that it didn't take him long to drop these good manners and these days he eats like a horse and with no restraint whatsoever!)

We decided to take Winston to the animal refuge the next day. Of course, this wasn't the best of prospects for a puppy, but still an improvement on dying from the cold in an old, abandoned cemetery. And we simply couldn't consider any other solution, because there was just no place in our life for a dog with a head shaped like a gherkin and with sticky-out ears and legs. However, my wife and I compromised on Winston staying this first night in our apartment. We built him a bed out of cushions and towels, onto which he got immediately and curled himself up into a neat ball. The dog closed his eyes without the faintest trace of mistrust. Which made me even more suspicious ... I had no idea whether dogs have a mind which they can use to ensure that a carefully planned project comes to fruition, but if this is the case, one thing seemed obvious: Winston wanted to stay right from the beginning and he had no doubt that no one could stop him, a certitude that enabled him to sleep soundly right from the first evening. The dog was there and we sensed his presence, even when he was curled up on his bed in the next room. From time to time, I crept up to his sleeping form and watched him: his long face, curved nose and closed eyes gave him something of the appearance of a mythical beast.

He also reminded me of the stock caricature of a crook or a smuggler, particularly when he opened his eyes a tiny little wicked crack, when he seemed to be grinning and enjoying his first small triumph, as if saying "I'm in and you're never going to get me out again." On this first evening, I did not yet know, but already had a dark suspicion that he was right.

WHAT DO YOU THINK HE WANTS?

Heartrendingly pathetic, sometimes even moving one to tears; the faces of abandoned and mistreated animals are amongst the most popular subjects in the media, apart from human catastrophes. There was the story of Lucky, a mongrel, who was found by a couple when he was wandering with a trailing lead on the Brenner motorway. At almost the same time, there was a news report about Gismo, a good-tempered Staffordshire terrier, whose callous owners had simply chained him to the gates of the animal refuge in Botnang, a case that called to mind the French bulldog, Ditsche, who was found tied to the entrance grille of the animal refuge in Dellbrück. These kinds of report always beg the question: how are people able to behave so heartlessly? A naive question, because humankind is clearly capable of letting its own children starve, or violate and even kill them.

An abandoned dog always generates a series of reactions. The finder rings the police; the police inform the animal refuge or place the dog – as fortunately happened in Lucky's case – with a trusted individual who will look after

WINSTON ...

the animal and may even home it permanently.
There are also dog owners who physically torture
their animals. Some time ago in Munich, the
police were involved in a case in which a woman
forced her German shepherd to stand in baths
full of cold water up to its stomach for hours at
a time. The dog was described as being scared;
the woman was prosecuted. In Remscheid, a
blind dobermann named Ishtar lives with a young
woman who saved the dog from being put to
sleep. Ishtar was previously at the mercy of an
owner who constantly mistreated her, finally
beating her so ferociously with a baseball bat
that Ishtar suffered a haemorrhage in one eye
and a detached retina in the other. An operation
failed to restore the dog's sight, and Ishtar
became totally blind. Love, understanding, and
other human virtues ensure that although Ishtar
can no longer see, she enjoys life in a loving and
comfortable environment.

Other stories that often also crop up in
relation to dogs are about them proving their
loyalty to their owners by covering distances
of hundreds of kilometres to find them again.
There was recently a report from Spain about
a dog that had died – or so everyone thought.
The owners buried the dog far away from the
village where they lived and sadly dedicated his
memorial. The day after the burial, the trusty dog
reappeared, looking a bit muddy, outside his
owner's front door; he had just been in a
state of suspended animation and
had dug himself out of his grave.

18

Spain is in general not a comfortable country for dogs, if the reports of hundreds of dog lovers are to be believed. The authorities there have a negligent and uncaring way of getting rid of stray dogs. Experts and critics have spoken openly about animals being gassed, hanged, or put to sleep unnecessarily. Any self-respecting dog lover either adopts a Spanish dog, or transports it – not without a certain amount of difficulty, expense and hardship, of course – to Germany, where the dog should first of all receive some psychological help. Fairly often on walks, when I ask other people where their dog came from, I am told: "We rescued him from a Spanish animal refuge." Rescuing a dog from certain death is a relatively easy exercise in humanity; everyone finds it easier to take a dog into their home rather than a Rwandan refugee. There is no reason, however, to moralise about this because dogs have their destinies, too, and the question of why someone is committed to helping dogs in need rather than desperate people is a pointless one.

The nature of the questions we asked ourselves after the first night with Winston was a lot less globally humanistic: had the dog been damaged by what had happened to him the previous evening? Have we spent the night with an animal whose soul is possibly ruined forever? Did Winston have nightmares? Was his psyche so disturbed by the experience of being abandoned that he would turn into a terrible killer dog, who would attack every human because he would see everybody in the same light as the person who had left him tied to a spindly tree in the cemetery?

In the morning, the dog stood in the living room on his bent, slightly wobbly legs and looked at us. What did he want? Perhaps he was thirsty, or perhaps he was asking for breakfast? He possibly needed a pee. The dog answered this question at once by squatting down and piddling on the parquet floor. We took him out for a walk immediately and, at that moment, introduced ourselves to the neighbourhood as dog owners. The dog ran, without seeming to have the faintest idea where he was going, pulling the lead from left to right and back left again. He didn't know what he was supposed to be doing apart from shivering with cold. Once he was back in the nice warm living room, he crapped on the carpet ...

We studied the vaccination card again and realised that this was issued on the same day that Winston's journey ended in the cemetery. So, on that Sunday, he must have first been taken for medical treatment and then immediately brought from Pilsen to Munich with the sole intent being to abandon him here. What can the reason for this have possibly been? Did a puppy broker plan to sell him and then the customer withdraw from the sale at the last minute? Was Winston a Christmas present who presented too many problems and needed to be got as far out of the way as possible to stop the dog returning to the family? It quickly became clear that these questions wouldn't get us any further, because the facts were there on the table as well as sitting short-legged and gherkin-nosed on the carpet: Winston was with us and what counted now was to find a solution for him

The Munich animal refuge, which my wife telephoned, agreed that it should have responsibility for him, but refused to take him as it was completely full. Just after Christmas was the busiest time and it was snowed under with abandoned dogs and those handed in by their owners; which meant that the space available for each animal became less and less, and the refuge was suffering an accommodation crisis. This was, of course, outrageous, and so we found ourselves in a moral dilemma: if we handed over Winston to the animal refuge, we would rid ourselves of a burden, but would burden our consciences. If we kept him, we would weigh down our entire lives. Conscience versus life: two seriously heavyweight issues standing in opposition to each other. I have no idea whether the dog was taking an interest in our arguments and deliberations; it's unlikely because, at that point, Winston suddenly discovered a hobby that he loves to this day: chasing his own tail. Whilst my wife and I were busy considering who in our circle of acquaintances would like a dog, Winston turned himself around like a spinning top with his open jaws trying to catch his black tail. It reminded me of a funny poem by Adelbert von Chamisso in which a rococo idiot takes offence at the fact that his pigtail always hangs behind him. The man turns round and round constantly, because he believes that this will at some point enable him to stop the pigtail hanging behind him. Winston went round and round, caught his tail and lost it again, whilst my wife rang a work colleague who she knew had owned a dog previously, and was looking for a pet for his young son. The man expressed a definite interest in adopting the dog, which could happen the following day.

So we could now say our goodbyes to Winston, the bow-legged, triangular-eyed karma canine that had been abandoned in an old cemetery, and who had narrowly escaped freezing to death during a cold Munich winter. That evening, after I had given the dog a manly, matey pat on his rear, my wife got Winston into the car, and I watched the pair of them go, slightly moved by the sight of the little dog skidding on the icy road, his bandy little legs constantly slipping. My wife heaved Winston into the car and that was that. From my vantage point at the window, I felt a short, moving episode come to an end, and the most important thing was that normal, dog-free life could now be resumed.

That evening and the next day, I told friends the story about the discovery of the dog. The story was greeted with amazement and smiles, anger about the cold-heartedness of the despicable individuals who abandoned the dog mixed with praise for our choice of name. No, we didn't give him the name Winston, I had to say at that point. It was written on his vaccination card. It's great that you managed to get rid of Winston, without him having to go to the animal refuge. Yes, that was a stroke of luck. It's really incredible how quickly you can get used to an animal if you don't act quickly enough, but you were quick enough, and will have forgotten about him in no time, especially as he's now in good hands.

When I got home, it still smelt slightly of the dog, and was a bit like the smell of a baby. I took apart his bed of cushions and towels to stop any sentimental feelings in their tracks. But that night I dreamt of Winston, although, unfortunately, the memory of Winston merged with that of my friend with the dog phobia. In short, I dreamt that Winston was roasted like a suckling pig and served up on a large plate: perhaps the dog had already got so deep into my consciousness that I couldn't excise thoughts of him? But daily routine would resume and the dog would prove to have been just a short break from that – or was the culinary dream a warning signal from my subconscious? Was it my duty to retrieve the dog because otherwise he would be in danger? After all, the dog had already been in a situation which could have proved fatal for him.

Despite my worries, however, over the next couple of days the memory of the long-nosed, strangely bowlegged dog began to pleasantly fade.

HE DOESN'T FIT WITH MY LIFESTYLE

Two evenings later, Winston was back again. I heard the rattle of his bowls on the stairway and caught myself feeling relieved. The door opened and the dog shot into the hallway, placed his paws on my lap and licked my hand. No, it wasn't at all the case that Winston was going to be staying just with us, my wife had arranged a joint venture with her colleague, a sort of dog-sharing arrangement. Winston would live with us for two days a week and stay the rest of the time with my wife's colleague, whom he had also completely accepted as an owner and who had also liked Winston a great deal. And early the next morning, my wife would take the dog with her to work – that had already been arranged – and Winston could even make himself useful as a therapy dog.

I had heard about dogs, cats and guinea pigs, and other small rodents, being used in old people's homes and psychiatric clinics to occupy the residents and patients, or, where possible, cheer them up. This form of therapy makes good sense, as any person damaged by life will chiefly blame his fellow men for his predicament. When you're trailing, tired and preoccupied with your thoughts up and down the corridors, or tramping in a depressed state around the clinic grounds, you just don't want anything more to do with humanity, and animals are the only possible source of contact and enjoyment in this situation, possibly even acting as rescuers. Arthur Schopenhauer, who believed the world to be a vale of tears, always walked around Frankfurt with a poodle, whose name was Atman, which is Sanskrit for 'principle of life' or simply 'breath.' If you are being stifled by life, you can catch your breath with a dog. Schopenhauer's affectionate nickname for Atman was 'Butz' (Fatty).

Winston's renewed presence forced me to re-adjust my attitude to him. It was still, of course, incontrovertible that proper everyday life was not possible with Winston. A dog just didn't fit with my concept of a life that was in many ways footloose and fancy-free and, well, short on responsibility. Aside from that, I wanted to continue to be in a position which enabled me to smirk at all the dog owners because the rhythm of their lives is aligned to such a great extent with that of their dogs. Something else, that didn't exactly disturb me, but which I did find unpleasant, were the very many virtues that owners ascribed to their dogs, of which loyalty is always the first to be mentioned. Loyalty was a word that made me shudder, because it suggested that the dog simply surrendered itself, for better or for worse, inevitably obliged to provide his master with 'better,' because 'worse' would undoubtedly be harder to put up with. Dreadful, how the presence of a dog suddenly forces you to confront fundamental moral issues head-on.

And obedience – an absolute requirement with dog ownership – was a concept for which I had never yet had any use. Obedience for me meant the old empire, subservience, at best National Service – and I didn't do that either. What, if on account of his bad experiences, Winston was now a completely ruined animal? Perhaps whoever had abandoned him had taught him some terrible habits that he was carefully hiding from us because he wanted to first ensure our loyalty. Maybe during that cold evening in the cemetery he had developed a fundamentally misanthropic attitude, which, once he was strong enough, would find some radical – or sinisterly subtle – form of expression against man. However, when I looked at Winston, there was absolutely no trace of negative characteristics of any kind.

He had an incredible energy, but was only able to use this for peaceful, if still destructive, purposes: he swept through rooms like a whirlwind, stopping intermittently to chew on table legs, rearrange the contents of the household rubbish bag, and then, as if to toast his achievements in the realm of interior design, pee on the carpet – every time. I had no idea whether as a dog gets older, he learns that furniture has a cultural function and is not meant for eating; or whether he is ready to understand that rubbish is there to be thrown away. Or could Winston's urge to shred rubbish in fact be a sign of intelligence, because the German word for rubbish is derived from the old High German word meaning to shred?

In the subsequent days and weeks of dog-sharing, Winston managed to end up spending the majority of his time with us. My wife bought a lead. She also purchased a new collar, to which we attached Winston's dog tag – his legal authorization making him a citizen of our city. And one day my wife came home with a little green checked cape which fitted the dog perfectly and gave him a slightly aristocratic, English air. So now we could be seen out and about with a coated dog. The overall effect of all these accessories with which we had kitted out Winston was to give him a certain status; he was now 'our dog;' even though my wife was still sharing the dog tax with her colleague, he had progressively less and less time for Winston, which meant that the dog now felt more and more at home with us.

It's about time I told you about the first few nights with Winston. These were, of course, winter nights, with everything that comes with that time of year around here: icy cold, snow, and hard-frozen mounds of snow at the edge of the streets. The dog's body wasn't regulated by an internal body clock, but instead by whatever need

WINSTON ...

was imminent at the time. We let Winston sleep in our room, which was my doing, not because I didn't want to miss out on being close to him at night – oh no, this was purely for commercial reasons, based on the fact that, if the dog went wandering around the apartment during the night, he would doubtless be making certain alterations to the furniture and floor coverings that could end up costing us a lot of money.

In the meantime, we had bought him a small basket, in which he lay down every evening in exactly the same position: rolled up like a snail shell, his muzzle buried under his paws. If he felt the light was left on too long, he pointedly put his paws over his eyes to draw attention to this intolerable situation. Then he went to sleep. Around three o'clock in the morning, with an additional option of either two or four o'clock, he got up and shook himself, which ensured that his collar and dog tag made a clattering, jangling racket. If you told him to lie down again, he set off his audible alarm system, which started with a short huff, and then stepped up to a more demanding woofing noise, before finally reaching its highest degree of intensity with barking that sounded and felt like the crack of a whip. That meant that he needed to go out, whether or not it was the middle of the night. And this meant that one of us had to get up, put on a jacket over our pyjamas, and go out into the street at some ungodly hour. However, as soon as he felt the icy cold of the winter night, he jammed his tail between his hind legs and refused to go onto the verge, which is where every dog in the neighbourhood did its business, bracing his front paws against the ground and looking at whichever one of us had the misfortune to be standing there, shivering, his eyes full of silent reproach: "How can you bring me out for this unpleasant night-time walk?" There had to be a good deal of tugging, cursing and swearing before Winston would do what he was supposed to and then go back to bed, laying down in his usual position, only to get up again about two hours later and ask for another night-time walk.

There were also nights when Winston did not have to satisfy any pressing physical need, but was instead troubled by persistent boredom, which he sought to overcome by means of shared playtime, coming to the bed with an arbitrary object in his mouth, such as a shoe or a belt, which he used as an invitation to a throwing or tugging game. A few hours later, he let us know it was time for his morning toilet, so at seven o'clock I was dressed in a strange amalgam of pyjamas and outdoor clothing, allowing my dog to walk in random zigzag fashion on his lead: I simply don't want to know how many grinning, dog-less people stood at their windows pitying the man who allowed the rhythm of his life to be dictated by a small, long-nosed dog.

WE REALLY SHOULD BE MORE DEFERENTIAL

In legal terms, Winston was the victim of a crime, and we could have tried to investigate his exact origins and involved the police, who would undoubtedly soon have caught up with the person who abducted him and abandoned him: according to statistics, 95 per cent of these kinds of violations of animal welfare legislation are resolved and punished with a heavy fine. But it never occurred to us for a moment to make Winston's case into a police matter. Very soon after the dog was found, a friend of mine declared somewhat fancifully though rather appositely: "The dog fell from a star and carefully selected exactly the two people who don't suit him at all." And it really does seem to me as if the fact that this dog found a home with us was a put-up job arranged by Winston himself.

The vet to whom we took Winston a couple of days after that cold Sunday evening was very impressed with his pedigree appearance and friendly temperament, but noted that he was not in good physical condition. The hours of standing in the snow had given him frostbite on his paws and full-blown pneumonia, two hardships with which, however, the pup coped easily. It was evident that he had not had enough to eat and we had to admit that he looked fairly emaciated.

His toughness helped him overcome this and, a couple of courses of antibiotics later, he was completely better. At the top of his left thigh, Winston had a tattoo, and a chip which wasn't registered, so no information was available that could throw any further light on his identity. At first, I often imagined that Winston had an ancient and noble lineage and was worth an unfeasibly large amount of money on the grounds of his pedigree. A bit like Kaspar Hauser, who was supposed to have been descended from the royal house of Baden. Perhaps his full name was Winston von Bohmen, or The Honorable von Pilsen, and if we sold him, young and healthy as he was, to a discerning breeder, we would be able to buy ourselves a detached house by Lake Starnberg with the proceeds.

The dog still didn't seem to belong to me, even when it became clear that my wife's work colleague didn't have any time to look after him. And so it came to pass that, after two weeks of rattling and panting at the door every evening, the dog burst in, jumped up to me and sank his sharp milk teeth into my wrist in a friendly manner. Winston was a constant presence, and his method of being present was absolute. When I sat at my desk, he demanded to also sit at the desk, and I had to lift him onto my lap where

he immediately began to chew and suck on my
fingers. If dogs appeared on the TV and barked,
Winston barked back conversationally. His desire
to communicate was unfailing, exceeded only
by his playfulness. Was there any possibility of
getting rid of the animal again? Could we sell him
to a dog-lover who had enough time to use strict
but humane methods to channel the craziness
of this dog to produce a well-behaved, obedient
companion trotting along on a lead?

My wife took note of my concerns and
enrolled Winston in puppy training classes. He
went every Saturday and, incredibly, quickly
learned the basic commands that every canine
must know, such as "sit" and "down." When told
to sit, Winston sat on his round, brown behind
and looked up, because in training class he had
learnt that he got something to eat if he did
this. When the command "down" was given, he
stretched out his front paws and lay down on the
ground, without altering his expectation that he
would be fed. However, despite the fact that he
would sit when told, Winston was still capable of
being completely undisciplined.

The destruction for which he was responsible
in the first few weeks and months was of a scale
that brought tears of rage to my eyes, a rage
that ran through my whole body, tormenting
the mercilessly vicious streak in a person and
threatening to enable it. How I would have liked

 to beat the living daylights out
of the dog after he got my
expensive, delicate spectacles

in his mouth and chewed them until
they were unrecognizable. There was a
terrible desire to inflict all manner of ills
on the animal after he chomped through
the laptop and telephone cables, and
chewed off the gearlever in the car
as if it were a stick of liquorice, but I
did nothing apart from swear terribly at
him. Although the number of functional
household gadgets was reducing on a daily
basis, I carried on giving him his brightly
coloured dry food, morning and evening, which
he ate in a matter of seconds. After every meal, I
took him out for walkies, although I felt incredibly
silly with a small, long-nosed dog on a lead,
collecting his deposits from the grass with the
help of black plastic bags, then keeping a furtive
look-out for a bin in which to get rid of the stuff.

Oh, how many clothes pegs have you
chewed and swallowed, Winston? How many
rugs have you crapped on and ruined, and
how many cushions have you shredded, not to
mention the soft toys that we were silly enough
to give you? How many peaceful nights have
you broken with your whip crack of a bark, and
how many shoes have you chewed to bits? And
let's not forget the damage you have done to our
nerves.

Now the dog was part of our everyday life
but I didn't want to concern myself with him.
Even so, if I had been asked at this point whether
or not I still wanted to give the dog away, my
answer would probably have been a little less

decisive than just weeks before. There comes a point when it's too late to give an animal away; after all, it gets used to its surroundings, and this long-nosed dog had already had a lot of unpleasant experiences. My arguments against Winston's banishment were essentially ethical ones, and that remark by my friend, Harald, about the planets from which Winston supposedly fell was actually serving as the basis of my championing of him. If others had disowned this dog, we were going to keep him as a stand against the baseness of the world, a defiantly humanistic attitude – flying in the face of reason. From the kitchen came the sound that Winston makes when he is eating plastic carrier bags ...

Then came a weekend when my wife had to go to a seminar. I saw her off with jokey advice about avoiding bringing home any more pets, and promised to do my utmost to take care of Winston. By now it was spring, and the cold that had nearly cut short the life of Winston the puppy had given way to much warmer weather. The right conditions for a walk, which I only wanted to do somewhere that I felt I would be virtually unobserved. I can't really explain it, but it was still embarrassing to me to be a dog owner. So I parked the car as close as possible to the English Garden and chose an area where I thought there would be very few people and dogs, particularly on a Saturday afternoon; and so it proved. Winston walked very sensibly on his lead and was generally relatively easy to manage. The nice thing about the English Garden is that every few metres there are very pretty little meadows, some of which are a bit hilly, others seeming to stretch as far as the eye can see, like on idyllic woodcuts from the 18th century. In one of these meadows, I unclipped the little carabiner clip that kept Winston tied to me for safety. I did this feeling somewhat anxious, because I was frightened that as soon as I set him free he would kick up his little bowed hind legs against his rear and disappear off through the meadow like a rabbit, running over the hill, along the footpath and then straight into the spokes of an ultra-light bike, whereupon I would immediately have to get the hotline of my insurance company on my mobile screen. It was indeed the case that Winston leapt about like crazy for a little while, particularly because he found the tall grass so interesting that he bounced up and down in it like a rubber ball, a sight which made me slightly regret that no one was there to appreciate this delicate acrobatic performance. But Winston didn't run away, instead turning round after every few steps because he wanted to ensure that I was staying close by. I called his name and ran a little way away from him. Immediately, Winston picked up his paws and bounced over as fast as he could.

In time, the technique of running away and then calling him developed into a game for which the dog's enthusiasm was fairly entertaining, and I would be fibbing if I denied that I also enjoyed it. I didn't restrain Winston from licking up a pigeon egg that lay in the grass, even though I didn't quite know whether that constituted poaching or not. Because he was excited, he crapped in the biotope, and I swear on my life that was the only time I haven't had one of those black plastic bags with me.

Interestingly, the running away game also worked in reverse. I jumped one pace towards Winston, he hopped one pace back; if I started to run towards him, he ran a few paces away. In those two hours, I suddenly got to know the dog. It was as if we had had an intimate conversation, but quickly broken this off in favour of lively distraction, and finally, wordlessly, and in complete agreement, decided on a life together.

WINSTON MAKES HIS ENTRANCE

It was now spring and high time that Winston began finding out that there were other dogs in the world besides him. I decided to take Winston to the dog park for the first time – that great green stage on which human and dog attest to their mutual closeness and affinity in such an adventurous way that the oddness of their pairing is all the more conspicuous. Tail wagging, Winston immediately introduced himself to various packs, greeted and was greeted by other dogs, checked out their ano-genital areas without any prior instruction, and had the same done to him. Every canine glance meant something specific, and every bark corresponded to a human thought.

I had no idea how Winston would behave in a meeting with his own species; in fact, I didn't even know if he regarded other dogs as his own species: until now, he had known only us. However, everything went swimmingly and after three or four meetings with strange canines, we had solid proof of Winston's social competence.

In my pre-dog days, I had witnessed how fights between dogs often transferred to their owners. Initially, wild barking is heard, after which the dogs throw themselves at each other, their owners trying to pull them off, all the while barking commands at the animals. This is then followed by mutual recriminations, whilst the dogs have completely forgotten their brief but violent attack on each other. I always had the feeling that the dogs were waging a type of proxy war; a physical confrontation that actually their masters were secretly wanting themselves. It may be that I'm just coming out with some kitchen table psychology here, but the theory is definitely an original one.

In tandem with the acceptance of my dog, I was also assessed for suitability by the owners, and must confess that there is scarcely anything more pleasant than the passing acquaintances among dog owners. The conversation initially centres on just one thing – the dog – although conversations often move on to general human matters, so that a whole new cosmos opens up for a dog park newbie.

One of my first new acquaintances was a young man with a fashionably shaved head and designer stubble, and a cheerful domestic life with his wife and friendly mongrel bitch, who was even taken on days out and holidays further afield. Their destinations of choice were the Mediterranean countries, particularly Italy, where the dog had especially liked Lake Garda, according to the man. The surprising thing for me was that this dog had obviously attained a degree of socialisation that enabled her to evaluate and appreciate the cultural aspects of Italy in their full glory, and possibly even to state a preference for other holiday destinations. In comparison, Winston seemed extremely stupid, at that very moment engaged in chewing on a dead mole.

There were not only dogs who had been rescued from animal shelters, but also those whose circumstances had undergone a complete change after their owners had split up – dogs from broken homes, as it were. I met one of these dogs together with his master, a young, very distinguished-looking man, who explained his dog's social situation to me as follows: "Initially, we thought that Jakob [the dog] wouldn't cope with the situation, but now he stays three days a week with Jutta and three days with me." (Not at all sure where Jakob went on the seventh day ...) I really had to admit that the dog was in impeccable condition, showed no sign of any strange behaviour and was therefore in no way a candidate for social services intervention. Instead, Jakob seemed the very epitome of a well-balanced hound.

I was told by another owner that his dog enjoyed a long walk through the wild area of the English Garden extremely early every morning, though then had to spend a good two hours by itself until the owner's wife could come to take care of it towards midday. Strangely, I felt it incumbent upon me to also make claims for Winston, inasmuch as this long-nosed dog was entertained all day long, and even did useful voluntary work in a therapeutic context at the hospital.

At this point, I must leave the subject of the dog park for a short while and quickly show you the open door to the hospital clinic, through which the dog bounded towards his friends every morning. His friends consisted of nursing staff and even patients, who sometimes knocked on my wife's office door and asked if the little dog was there again, and whether he could possibly come for a walk? Within a very short time, Winston had managed to make a few very gloomy patients laugh, just with his normal antics, which consisted of hopping like a rabbit, running, slowing down too late and crashing into the door, putting his paws into laps and licking hands.

Right from the beginning of our participation in events at the dog park, the following natural law was obvious: when the dogs are enjoying a boisterous game, the owners really get on well; Winston once met a Jack Russell terrier, who rushed up to him full of energy and desperate for a chase, and involved him in a wild game which was quite demanding, even for Winston. The Jack Russell's owner and I watched a high level trial of strength, a superior natural spectacle, in which two canine bodies flew through the air, shot across the closely mown grass like medium-range missiles, and raced so close past their owners that fractures to the lower leg region were avoided by only a whisker.

"Completely immersed in their game,"

concluded Jack Russell man. "And no trace of
aggression," he continued, enthusiastically. I
endorsed his analysis and we both continued our
entranced observation of the craziness unfolding
before us. Then we got around to discussing
the difficulty of finding the right playmates
for our dogs. I found that most dogs that we
met in the parks of Munich were too slow and
feeble for Winston, boring old fat canines who
just trotted along and made no effort to romp
around. Jack Russell man acknowledged this
problem: "I told the owner of a Scottish terrier
that there was no point in letting our dogs play
together. Everything took far too long and my
dog just needs exercise." I admired Jack for his
frankness: "All play, zero aggression" repeated
Jack Russell man. I nodded in agreement, and
we returned happily to our cars, some one and a
half hours later.

Shortly after the meeting with the Jack
Russell, Winston met a rather large black dog
carrying a red frisbee in its mouth, owned by a
woman who, to my mind, was dressed a little
too smartly for the dog park. The black dog, by
contrast, emanated a guiltless, lazy nastiness.
He was rude to Winston, who mistook the
jostling for a game, and suddenly found himself
right underneath the huge black creature. My
dog squealed like a pig which caused the black

monster to graciously let him go – but Winston took off, running as if the devil incarnate was after him; who knows, to Winston, perhaps this black creature was indeed the devil in dog form? Winston paid no attention to my shouts – he was running for his life, that much was obvious. With increasing horror, I watched his progress across the field, saw how he turned right – the direction from which we had come – and then disappeared. I began to run myself with the vision of walkers fleeing in panic from the dog racing towards them. I already saw Winston dashing along the gravel path by the Eisbach, onto the road and straight into an over-polished BMW. I ran with no hope of being able to salvage anything, but after about a hundred metres, I found him again.

Panting heavily in the middle of the pavement with tongue lolling, Winston had discovered that some dogs had it in for him; dogs who showed him that life is full of danger. Winston had seen the bad side of dogs, and was already fed up to the back teeth with it.

THE PERSON SHOULD COME TO THE DOG

I had no idea how to train a dog, and must add that my desire to have any kind of educational effect on Winston was very small. There was much that he was not yet ready to learn as he was still very young, and when I looked at other dogs, many were not as easy to manage as Winston. Nonetheless, these kinds of comparison did not compensate for the fact that Winston's presence had thoroughly shaken up our world like a whirlwind.

In most books or films about dogs, the animal – with his jaunty joie de vivre – brings a breath of fresh air into the tediousness of human everyday life; but our everyday life wasn't at all tedious and if we had ever needed any fresh air, we had found that opening the window was perfectly adequate for our needs. We really had had no need for Winston, honestly not. We could have gone on perfectly well as we were; carrying on our relatively low-key life, pleasantly coloured by travel, visits to restaurants, and work.

There are those – and they should in no way be ridiculed – who view a dog as a social being, and frequently enjoy their company more than that of a fellow human. Of course, this is nothing to object to and if you look at the majority of people in these terms, deciding to get a dog is completely logical. But this should be voluntary; the person should get a dog and not the other way round. Of course, we liked the dog, perhaps we even loved him, if you can use this word for the affectionate bond between human and animal. But both of us, my wife and I, would have been happy if this dog had not sought us out. If my wife had taken another route that Sunday evening in January, the dog would undoubtedly have frozen to death. But we wouldn't have known of his fate. A council worker would have put the stiff, frozen body of the little puppy in a plastic bag and driven it to the specialist waste disposal facility. Perhaps there would have been a little report in the local news section of the newspaper two days later, but I probably wouldn't have even read the whole thing.

The dog starts barking early in the morning. He wants to go out and he wants something to eat. He needs exercise that I don't – at least not at seven o'clock in the morning. There are things lying around in our living room that look ridiculous and whose function I am embarrassed to explain to visitors: fragments of the soles of shoes, a bone made of different coloured threads, a headless rubber chicken, a plastic wheel, which, when operated skilfully, disgorges chunks of food. But Winston doesn't do skilful operation. Everything that he gets hold of is

broken: spectacles, plants and cushions. He eats our food off the table and helps himself to onions and garlic cloves from the larder.
The dog is insatiable and shameless. He is almost uncontrollable and really should have been put to sleep. But no vet puts a healthy dog to sleep. Aside from that, you'd then have to deal with all the animal rights people, the ones who demonstrate against the conditions in Spanish animal shelters.

At some point, I began to buy dog books. The list of manuals on training and behaviour is as long as the Great Wall of China. There are titles like *Talk to Dogs, Knitting for Dogs, Calming Signs for Dogs, Fun Nose Games for Dogs, The Big Book of Games for Dogs, Species-Appropriate Raw Food for Dogs* and *Understanding Dogs Properly*. The astrologist and dog expert Jeanne Philippi produced the astrological companion *My Dog and His Stars*, and American zoologist Elizabeth Marshall Thomas believes in all seriousness that dogs humanize themselves to the extent that they copy our smile: "When around people, these dogs pull their lips back grotesquely in order to bare their teeth and so look like us," she writes in her book *The Secret Life of Dogs*. You can get to thinking some strange thoughts when you sit for hours and hours in front of a dog and watch what he's doing ... Mrs Marshall Thomas really should have read Konrad Lorenz's lovely book *Man Meets Dog*, written in the 1950s,

in which he gives a clear explanation that the
behaviour described above is actually merely the
preliminary stage of panting. Yes, I had ended
up in the land where panting was the norm.
And my job here was not head of government,
but chauffeur and bodyguard, because Winston
had to be constantly entertained, supervised
and driven somewhere. To the vet, for example,
who at some point stopped charging us for the
treatment; we paid only for the medication.
Winston suffered from colds, rashes, and coughs,
and once he even had to have an operation, but
I'll tell you more about that later.

The dog was not just astonishingly
greedy, he also jumped up at everybody who
approached him in a friendly manner, which is a
habit he still has. And when his big, Roman nose
detected some food in a stranger's bag, he didn't
hesitate to stick this nose into the

bag. No one used to normal
social conventions likes this
kind of behaviour, but how do
you train an animal out of his
pushiness and bad manners?

I began to look for dog training schools on
the internet. These all had one thing in common:
they advocated non-violent training. I have to
admit that Winston's training has not always
been completely non-violent, if you can really
term the despairing efforts to which I resorted
in order to protect my nerves violence. I have
certainly always been aiming for the best possible
outcome when I clouted the dog – not very

hard – on the back with a rolled-up TV listings magazine, and have given him a slap for being a cheeky rascal. I put a muzzle on him when his fidgeting escalated into knocking chairs over and pulling tablecloths onto the floor. I steered clear of electric shock collars and water sprays because these remind me of the methods used in some torture chamber somewhere in Latin America. I shouted at the dog, which had a more immediate effect than whacking him, but no long-term efficacy.

At some point, I was given the tip of talking to the dog in a very soft voice, rather than thwacking him or shouting at him. I breathed his name, whispered my request to him to stop biting the returnable plastic drinks bottle, because returning the bottle meant receiving cash, from which he, Winston, would also profit in the form of dog food, and I accompanied these explanations with stroking his egg-shaped head. It helped. The dog was so surprised by the mildness of my tone, that he stopped what he was doing and let go of what he had in his mouth. Of course, he soon saw through the whispering method as a variant of my helplessness disguised as authority and returned to his carefree and limitless chomping activities.

It is always said that dogs provide just enough balance in people's lives to ensure that they are needed. The dog is not just a social partner, but an actual therapeutic remedy, whose wagging tail triggers a healing response in his master's soul. With this in mind, many tenancy disputes have been resolved in favour of dog owners. A dog-phobic apartment owner has no chance of giving notice to his much-disliked dog-owning tenant if the latter can prove that his rottweiler is the foundation of his spiritual and mental wellbeing.

With the best will in the world, no one could say that Winston is a therapeutic remedy; rather an aggressive neurotoxin that leads to irritation and occasional bad-temperedness. Sometimes I worry that, contrary to the theories posited by animal lovers, Winston is going to shorten my life by a few years. This is down to the inner conflict that he causes me. Because, of course, as an ethically inclined and sympathetic person, I want Winston to have a long and happy life. A nice sentiment, but what does it mean for me, for my wife, for us? That this life will be long and happy with us, in our guardianship and with our money. And 'long' for dogs of this size means fifteen years. I'll be in my mid-fifties by this time and presumably, because of my self-sacrificing work for Winston, I will look like I'm in my early sixties.

A QUESTION OF TRAINING — AND EAR CARE

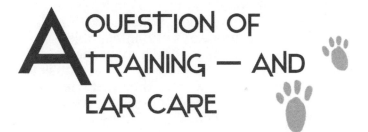

Anyone who goes out and about with a dog can count on always having a wide variety of acquaintances; the very reason, of course, why old and lonely people get themselves a mutt. If you look around the city and in the usual dog-meeting places, you will soon find proof that many people are incredibly lonely because the number of dogs tells a very clear statistical story.

Over the course of a year, I've got to know many dog owners. Elderly ladies, who let themselves be chased around by their torpedo-like Jack Russell terriers; children who were walked by Golden Retrievers, and old men, who anxiously picked up their poodles when a larger dog appeared. Suddenly, I was in the company of Great Danes with pendulous flews standing next to me, Shar Peis displaying their disturbingly exotic looks, Bull Mastiffs who minutely examined my shoelaces, and a Dobermann that temporarily took on the job of looking after Winston. This occurred when, together with Winston, I met a group of young people who were very keen on dogs, and who were always dying to ask – but luckily never did – how much

WINSTON ...

I would sell him for. (And just to clarify once and for all: not at any price. Winston, with all his funny, captivating ways and intolerable awfulness, is ours.) Be that as it may, the Dobermann, a quiet, elderly dog, felt responsible for Winston from the moment they met. He even took on the role of father or benevolent grandfather, by allowing himself to be involved in Winston's loutish games. But then something happened which the Dobermann clearly felt was not funny. Suddenly, as if from nowhere, a belligerent mongrel appeared in the dog park and targeted Winston, who had no experience of fighting, by pouncing on him and pestering him with various types of unruly behaviour. The Dobermann watched perhaps two of these forays discontentedly, but when the intruder came back a third time, he chased him off, barking until he had left completely. The Dobermann was rewarded – rightly so, in my opinion – with great recognition of his educational input, and was petted and stroked, even by me, albeit somewhat cautiously. Because although I am now out and about in the local area with my own dog, I have still not got a completely natural relationship with other canines. I watch in wonder and respect as a person, who Winston doesn't know at all, strokes my dog's muzzle with both hands and even risks cuddling him. In a beer garden we once met a man who – rather stupidly in my opinion – summoned up the courage to confidently put his hand in Winston's mouth. What if the dog had suddenly bitten down on it? Would the insurance company have paid up or would it have said that it was the man's fault, because you shouldn't go around putting your hands in dogs' mouths? If I do something like this myself, then that's a completely different matter: Winston knows me and I know Winston, but I don't know other dogs and they will probably remain strange to me forever.

I was connected with the owners of all of these animals for what were almost always fleeting but very pleasant minutes. The conversation obviously centred exclusively on dogs, in particular Winston, whose smart appearance and comic playfulness prompted appreciation and amusement. Of course, I joined in with the praise and said nothing about the trouble this dog caused me. "He's a very lively dog," as we say in diplomatic dog owner speak. And this assessment was in no way incorrect. I have heard it said that there are men who get themselves extra muscular dogs to enable them to attract women. I view this as a complete non-starter because the dog park is as far removed from the erotic sphere as the Great Dane is from the Yorkshire Terrier. The main priority here is to prevent any sexually-related behaviour, in particular mounting other dogs, a behaviour that is also an exhibition of dominance among dogs and always requires the owner to intervene. In fact, relatively little can happen in this situation, but there are dog owners who see the mounting behaviour of other dogs as morally objectionable. I'm talking about the type of people who feel that, in addition to their own dog, they have to train my dog and the dogs of other people. The owner of a Golden Retriever rebuked another woman whose dog mounted the Retriever. She said that she didn't see why she should have to tolerate this canine intimacy, and that it was a matter of training whether or not a dog acted in this pushy way. This woman helped me realise that there is a kind of dog owner who inhabits, shall we say, an intellectual grey area ...

The woman who had been reprimanded countered by saying that dogs made these kinds of advances to one another, and then added the nice, clever and frankly obvious statement: "But this is what makes them animals, not people." As regards Winston, the morally upright dog owner merely remarked that his ears weren't clean enough and should be carefully cleaned out with a wad of cotton wool. There is advice for which I am grateful and then there is this kind of advice for which I am not grateful at all.

These are animals and not people, a rule, as obvious as it may sound, that's a bit less clear-cut for anyone who frequents a dog park. Almost every dog owner is immutably convinced of their knowledge of the character, basic personality traits, and preferences of his or her animal. Amy growls at all young dogs, and so, for her mistress, she is an elderly lady who likes a peaceful life. A Boxer has been called 'Granddad' since birth and is therefore treated with appropriate care. When the Greyhound suddenly turns away from the ball, the owner

says: "We're going home soon." But the animal
didn't say anything.

One afternoon, I was walking with Winston
in the English Garden, for the most part engaged
in trying to stop Winston from hunting. Well-
meaning, dog-owning acquaintances had warned
me about the fine of seventy euros if a dog dug
up mole hills. As Winston did not know that mole
hills are protected architectural monuments,
or have any awareness of the value of seventy
euros, he was busily engaged in digging with
his forelegs, soil flying out between his hind
legs; it was a pleasant sight, because it gave the
impression of useful activity, even enthusiastic
work. The dog wanted to hunt a mole – what
could really be wrong with that? When the Parks
Department comes through the park with its
mowers, there is a hideous massacre of the
burrowing creatures. I'm always having to extract
mangled moles from Winston's jaws.

In any case, on this particular afternoon,
one of these already destroyed molehills was
Winston's unexpected undoing. Whilst looking for
his tennis ball – a fetish-type exercise which I will
explain with an example later – Winston caught
his foreleg in a mole hole and fell flat on his face.
As he wobbled slowly to his feet, I could see that
he was limping. Winston was hobbling so much
that he lay down every few steps,
and I began to fear that he had
broken something. Apart from
the dog's suffering, I was
already worrying about

WINSTON ...

my bank balance as a compound fracture, which
would necessitate an operation, costs several
hundred euros. Winston tried twice to walk, but
then gave up and lay in the grass, looking at
me mournfully. Of course, I knew exactly what
the dog wanted me to do, and it was perfectly
clear to me that I would have to do it if I still
wanted to get to my car and drive home today.
So I picked up Winston and carried him like a
wounded soldier from the green battlefield. As
I got closer to the pavement, I saw two elderly
ladies, one of whom was holding her hand in
front of her mouth. She put her hand down and
called to me: "What's wrong with the baby?"
The baby? I only had Winston with me, of whose
complete and utter dogginess I had, until this
point, been completely convinced. Winston was
indeed relatively small and perhaps six months
old. As I approached the women with the injured
Winston, they gave me all sorts of advice
about how to deal with this kind of leg injury in
babies. I couldn't remember the names of all the
ointments, drops and baby doctor addresses;
there were too many of them. Nevertheless,
I thanked them and hauled the dog back to
the car and drove home, where, in his normal
carefree manner, he raced around the rooms
without the faintest hint of a limp. Winston had
just not wanted to walk all the way back from
the dog park to the road on his own four feet,
and had therefore pretended an injury. Babies
are just not that sly or bright – only a damn dog
could do that!

WORK ON THE DOG

Sometimes I visit the dog park very early in the morning, and then I can't resist a spot of natural romanticism. When we, Winston and I – obviously, I'm already talking about Winston as if he is my partner – enter the field, there is still mist lying on the grass, and I imagine that it is our, particularly Winston's, task to rip the veil from this fresh morning with one powerful movement, so that we can start our walk in the landscape of Eichendorff's lyrical romanticism. At moments like these, for a couple of minutes I think how nice it would be to only be involved with dogs: Winston already takes up most of my day, so I could give up my job – which is subject to the daily grind of the office and therefore a little boring from time to time – and dedicate myself completely to the training and study of dogs. Then I would have this and other intense experiences of nature every morning, have healthy colour in my cheeks, wild, shoulder-length hair and a fashionable, three-day old beard, which would identify me as a weatherproof but kindly loon, who got on better with dogs than with people.

WINSTON ...

However, the early morning in the dog park can't be that early as we still see other 'mummies' and 'daddies' with their furry 'babies.' Why do people always assume their dogs can only understand baby language, as though they can't accept a master or mistress but, instead, have to have a 'mummy' or 'daddy.' Dogs have 'biccies,' 'go to beddy–byes,' and do 'poo–poos.' Once Winston jumped up at a young man, who then gently asked my dog to stop doing jumpies. On another occasion, Winston bit the same man's fingy-wingy, because he was rumbly in his tumbly, apparently, as the young man had previously applied some rose-scented hand cream. I apologised profusely for the bite, which luckily hadn't drawn blood, and was left full of admiration for a man who had already got around to applying rose-scented hand cream at six o'clock in the morning.

At around the same time, an elderly gentleman is always out with me in the early morning dew, with his dog that looks as if it is home-knitted and, although somewhat younger than Winston, is three times as big as he is. The dog answers – although somewhat infrequently – to the name of Leo and loves to dance its heavy, matted self about in front of Winston and then get chased by him, whilst Winston prefers to be the one who is chased, so the game is quickly re-directed to his liking. The sociable Leo is a nice example of a completely disobedient dog, as he always ends up a good distance away from his master, which his master finds exhausting.

Once, I told Leo's boss that I was considering taking Winston to dog training school, which prompted the man to explain that he didn't reckon much to these kinds of places because they changed the character of the dog. At that point, I was sceptical about the man's view, though these days agree with him one hundred per cent – and I'll be treating you to an extensive explanation of why later on. At any rate, the relationship between master and dog is, to a greater degree, based on the following premise: "The dog has to love you," as the man said whilst we both stood looking into the distance where the enormous Leo was barely a small, black and white dot.

Dog owners are at their most interesting when they have to work out their role in a pack. Masters and mistresses often stand in a semi-circle around dogs that are playing wildly together, and sometimes it is they, rather than the dogs, who decide who can join in. A certain young German Shepherd keeps being removed because there is something not quite right about his behaviour. As far as I can see, there is nothing to differentiate him from the other dogs in terms of his behaviour and desire to play, but he seems destined to permanently bring out the worst in the characters of well–trained mongrels – or perhaps he simply has an image problem. Balls are thrown and removed from the jaws of dominant dogs and gently rolled in front of smaller, less assertive dogs, because they should have their chance, too. The injustice of the world, the sad fact that there are winners and losers – all this is rectified at the dog park.

Some dogs need – as I have so often heard from owners – 'to work,' just as some people need to work with each other on their partnership or on themselves. Presumably, no close relationship, other than that between husband and wife, has so much importance attached to it as does the relationship between human and dog. This is also logical, as we can only be separated from the dog by death – preferably that of the dog. There is no divorce, no temporary separation, or any other cowardly rearguard action as there is in human relationships. And because this is the case, the relationship with the dog must be finely balanced. There should be as few problems as possible, which, of course, never happens, though perhaps the comparison to children – which is very unpopular amongst educated people – does actually fit here. Dog owners who say that their dogs are their children, or, more moderately, that they are like their own children, are regarded as intellectually a bit suspect. Moreover, animal psychologists advise against the idea that dogs could replace the unfulfilled desire for children. These animals, so we read time and again in books and articles written by experts, are condemned to be humanized in a way that conflicts with their nature, and is likely to turn the animals into nervous wrecks.

However, it is still the case that dogs do the same irritating things that children do: they never do what we tell them to, they take what they want, and they cause offence in public, although I was happy to discover that, in Germany, dogs are a great deal more popular when out in public than are children. When I go into a butcher's and tie Winston outside the door on the dog hook embedded in the wall, he starts to make a huge racket. He yowls and barks and tries to break loose, so a few people who wanted to buy a bit of meat decide they would rather keep their distance, and perhaps even become vegetarian. In spite of this, the butcher's wife gives me a little pork sausage with my shopping "for the good little doggy" who, in fact, had not been the slightest bit 'good' but a right royal painy in the arsey, as usual. But, for the business-minded butcher, every dog is good and the reward for acknowledging this notional 'goodness' is the best advertising.

There are bowls of water for dogs everywhere; there are sometimes sweets for children at the till, but the children can't get to them. One thing is true, though for both children and dogs: they need proper training. There is a bigger range of dog training courses, dog training schools and dog training methods than there is of children's nurseries. During the first few months of his life, Winston visited a puppy training school which used playful methods to introduce the dog to life. There he learnt, as I have already mentioned, the magic words Sit and Down, which he still assumes to be synonymous with the promise that there will be something to eat right away. Winston was in no way dimmer than the other little dogs at the puppy school. He just got bored more quickly and tended towards loutish behaviour when there was any discipline in the lesson.

On one occasion, all the dogs and their trainers and masters and mistresses went on a trip to a pond. The other dogs appreciated the coolness of the water, but not Winston. He discovered a dead frog on the bank of the pond, which he ate without any formalities. He had yet again given a vivid demonstration that the consumption of food has to be prioritised above any moral or educative value. And in so doing, he had also yet again demonstrated that he is an animal: an animal – and not a person.

Breeds of Owner

It's about time that we drew up a list of the breeds of owner to stand alongside the various breeds of dog. To any fans of political correctness: please don't make a fuss – breeds of owner is just a fun expression and we're going to be stubborn and hang onto it. We have already got to know some masters and mistresses, and a few of them have even become friends, but there are others we have avoided because their narrow-mindedness and incorrigible nature mean that we just can't get on.

One such individual is an elderly man in our road who, when I appear on the pavement with Winston, crosses to the other side of the street, or even goes in the opposite direction, because he is convinced that Winston would kill his ugly little poodle by jumping on him and breaking his back. This poodle really is a very repellent creature, because even when he is twenty metres away from Winston he throws himself on the ground. His owner obviously has a perversely exact idea of what dogs of

WINSTON ...

Winston's calibre would do to dogs like his silly poodle. On one occasion, I made clear to the old man – admittedly somewhat indignantly – that Winston had about six times more character than his ratty little beast, but to be honest this was expressing far too much in terms of emotion. There are people who divide everything in the world into decent and offensive; categories that they consistently apply to the canine world, where they lie around alien and useless, because dogs simply don't conform to these kinds of classification.

There exists a large and militant group of dog owners who are fundamentally unhappy with their own lives and therefore have a preference for very unhappy dogs. They are always looking at web sites which have pictures of hanged dogs, or those that have been intentionally torn apart by wild animals, or tied to the back of a car by sadistic owners and dragged to death along stony country roads. Stored in their 'favourites' menu they have sites like Cocker Spaniel Rescue, Bull Terrier Rescue, and everything that has to do with dogs in need of rescue. On these sites, you find short biographies of dogs who have had a sad life. The pathetic thing about these texts is that they are written from the point of view of the dog, as if it is writing directly to the heart of his future owner: "My name is Jago, I am about four years old and have not had much in the way of good luck in my short life. My first master had no patience with me, impetuous little guy that I am, and kept hitting my paws with his slipper when

I'd made a little mess in his living room. Aside from that, he gave me so little to eat that I got very thin and the people from the animal refuge had to put me in a home. My second master got me from there and he was much nicer than my first one. But, sadly, he couldn't cope with my madcap ways and after six months I was back in the animal refuge. Now I am looking for a nice master or mistress who has a big garden and an even bigger heart. But you must have some experience of dogs as sometimes I am not very easy to deal with. I get on well with children if they are not too young, but don't really care for cats."

These little monologues are great denouncements of our world, poisoned as it is by violence and injustice. The people who write these can't find the actual courage to raise their voice against this, or perhaps, with their anger at all the wickedness, they don't know where to start, and so lend their voice to the dog, who tells of his lot in life in emotive terms that go straight to the reader's heart, every time.

There is a fringe group, luckily very small, which is made up of dyed-in-the-wool misanthropists, who withdraw from other people and have the attitude that only a dog is a true friend because he has no guile or cunning and is therefore completely free of human malevolence. The humorous, but nearly forgotten essayist, Sigismund von Radecki, once wrote about this type of affection for animals that it smacked of reverse misanthropy, and he went on: "How stupid would a dog then have to be to worship people!"

At this time a private visit took me to Vienna, where I met my friend from China, who had hoped that his meal of dog meat would liberate him from his dog-bite trauma. However, the meal had not had any long-term effect as he was still frightened of dogs; a fear which seemed very deeply ingrained – far deeper than a canine tooth could reach into flesh. What was worthy of reporting about my visit to Vienna was, however, not the visit to see my dog-eating friend, but, on the contrary, a meeting with a woman whose love of dogs had taken on such dimensions that it could perhaps only be checked by intensive therapeutic input, if at all.

It was Austria's National Day and the Austrian army had assembled for a splendid military ceremony in the Heldenplatz. I'm not a great admirer of soldiers and their performances, so instead I was observing the people who were watching the parade. Suddenly, in amongst the crowd, I saw a woman with two small dogs of the same sort as Winston. Cheered by this sight, I went over to the woman and spoke to her about the dogs. She was Russian and spoke only very poor German, and after some initial distrust – perhaps she thought I was from the veterinary inspection office and wanted to check her dogs – she started to chat to me by first asking me whether I was married. She herself was not – or rather, not any more and was therefore looking for a husband. She was going to have a meeting with a prospective candidate shortly, whom she had made contact with via a personal ad. But she didn't think anything was going to come of it because all her relationships so far had foundered because of the dogs. And it wasn't as if the two white bull terriers were her only dogs. She also had a pointer at home and the domestic scene was completed by three cats. At least every five minutes the Russian woman said the sentence that I had been expecting since the start: "They are all my children."

Her life had really gone down the tubes because of her pathological love of animals. She had been thrown out of her apartment, and now lived in a tiny flatlet with the animals, three of which – the dogs – slept in her bed with her. Of course, she would adopt more dogs, she said, because the world is full of persecuted dogs. She talked about circumstances in the canine world as if a special type of fascism focused on canine persecution had broken out in Europe, and as if it were necessary to provide shelter to a huge number of persecuted dogs, whenever and wherever you could.

The woman told me about networks in which she was involved. In the near future, she would probably also scrape together the last of her money and travel to Spain, where there were also dogs who had fallen on terribly hard times and needed rescuing. She asked whether I was married in the vain hope that she could curtail her search for a man on the spot and abandon the pending meeting with the contact from the personal ad. When I said yes, she said that I was too young for her anyway and got out her mobile and spent another half an hour showing me pictures of her dogs in every conceivable situation. I was afraid I would never get away from her and began looking for an escape. Luckily, eventually the need to keep her appointment with the eligible bachelor became pressing, and she disappeared with her bull terriers into the teeming mass in the Heldenplatz.

This is how far things can go if you lose all sense of reserve with your own dog, when the dog conquers areas central to human life so that, in the end, there is no longer any difference between the everyday life of human and dog. People like the Russian woman in the Heldenplatz condemn themselves to leading a dog's life. Since meeting her, I have been worried: how do you notice when you are crossing the boundary between normal and pathological love of animals? Is it perhaps an inevitable road to ruin when you adopt a dog and schedule your time so that you are satisfying him and his needs as broadly as possible? What are the warning signals that you should call a halt before it's too late? When the dog sleeps next to the bedside rug? When he sleeps next to his master in bed? Or not until he is sleeping in his master's bed instead of his master, who has to live in the kennel, like in Loriot's glorious dog cartoons? Had we done everything correctly with Winston, or is he already taking up too much space in our life?

WE HAVE TO TALK — ABOUT YOUR DOG

Complete strangers have explained to me in the greatest possible detail what my dog is like and what he should be like. Dog training, like every educational subject, gives rise to various types of expert, and I had cause to get to know more than I really wanted to. I have already mentioned the more entertaining experts, who give me private tips about how to solve or reduce some or other canine problem. I now know how to clean Winston's ears like an expert and how to deal with his occasional diarrhoea without having to consult a vet. I was told about the many different remedies for inflammation of the paw pads by a woman with decades of experience of using Fuller's Earth. I also already know which vet to go to if Winston should ever fall victim to the dreaded eye dislocation. But there are a couple of things I still don't understand: how to make the dog comprehend that chair legs are not a foodstuff; and that strangers are not generally going to be pleased when a young dog expresses its excitement by putting muddy paw prints on their trouser legs. How can I drum it into Winston's head that he is supposed to walk next to me on his lead and not charge ahead, pulling me along like a torpedo on a chain?

At the beginning, I believed I could get the answers to all these questions from those people who deal with dogs at a professional level. I have a lot of respect for experts, precisely because I am not one myself. I never doubted that the employees and operators of dog–sitting services and dog training schools knew the canine psyche as thoroughly as the dog knows his olfactory environment.

One day, my wife's workplace changed to another hospital clinic where she couldn't take the dog, so we had to find an alternative place for Winston to stay during the day. The first address that I selected was a type of day-care centre for dogs, which made a really good first impression. It was staffed by young people who spent their whole day helping dogs of various different breeds to while away their time. The animals were assembled into groups and involved in games of skill, set little tasks, and could race around outside in the fenced garden. The afternoon playtime was rounded off with an hour's walk, so in short, the whole thing was paradise and even accommodated Winston's leisure-focused interests.

At first, the arrangement worked really well, Winston made no fuss when we left him there, and didn't even look around at me when I hung up his lead on the hook and disappeared in the direction of the office. I felt that I had got the dog engaged in some educationally useful activities for a few hours, thereby buying myself some precious time for me and my daily work. In the evening, I picked up Winston, chatted to the duty dog carers about his impetuous but friendly nature, and then drove home. Winston always fell asleep during the drive and remained in a tolerably dopey state all evening. There could be no more suitable solution, no happier combination between proximity and distance: I was as relieved as a single father, who had finally found a nursery place for his son. Of course, Winston was a wild child and his cheeky ways took some getting used to, but he really didn't mean any harm and, when all is said and done, who is more likely to understand a playful pup than a trained dog-sitter? After a couple of weeks, the manager of the dog day-care centre took me aside one evening and explained to me – regretfully, and in the manner of a sympathetic but strict nursery school teacher – that the girls, ie the students, didn't want to work with Winston any more. The reason for this was that Winston was absolutely not prepared to accept his lowly position in the pack, and instead insisted on being a leader, a position to which he was not entitled. In brief, she said that the dog was not capable of subordinating himself to dog society which had its own strict rules. Winston would no longer hand over the tennis ball that he constantly carried around in his mouth, and if another canine wanted to carry the ball for a while, Winston became bad-tempered. Moreover, he was so wild and energetic that it

WINSTON ...

was scarcely possible to have any control over
him. Furthermore, he wasn't prepared to give
the carer allocated to him any opportunity to get
involved with other dogs, regarding the woman
as his personal assistant, whose services he
wasn't about to share.

This conversation was obviously very
unpleasant for me, because it cast me in the
role of a father at a school parents' evening.
The dog day-care centre manager assumed
the role of concerned teacher, who painted a
picture of a pupil that could only be described
as disastrous, if not hopeless. It sounded as if
Winston's position there was acutely endangered.
I came to an agreement with the centre manager
that I would only bring Winston there one day
a week from now on. The rest of the time, he
would just have to spend alone in our apartment.
Unfortunately, this did not result in a reduction in
the number of complaints, however, as I received
an ever chillier reception from the students
when they handed Winston to me at the
end of every day that I left him in the
centre. The whole thing became more
and more embarrassing for me every
time, and when one day Winston had
chewed up the handbag belonging
to one of the girls, I decided to
keep him away from the centre
for good. In recompense for the
handbag, which was a pretty
hideous one, I pressed twenty
euros into the girl's hand – an

expense that I am still irritated by today. The dog
fell asleep in the car during the journey home,
exhausted by the demands of his day, which had
ensured that he remained in full possession of
his ball, even if the price for this had been a high
one: avoidance of a subordinate position in the
pack which had then resulted in exclusion from
the dog day-care centre.

Whilst I drove home, looking from time to
time at the snoring dog lying in the footwell,
my disappointment about Winston's alleged
misbehaviour gradually transformed into at first
restrained and then ever more powerful pride. Of
course: the dog was like me: volatile, stubborn,
and not prepared at any price to subject himself
to a hierarchy in a ridiculous – you might even
say abject – system. This was because Winston
was Winston and not Fifi, Amelie or Goofy. He
was Sir Winston, the dog who came from the
Czech Republic, had sat for hours in the snow
and suffered frostbite and survived pneumonia.
Winston the dog who managed to drive a quiet,
calm married couple completely crazy; Winston
who showed no respect for nicely crafted
furniture and spectacles. Exactly why should this
Winston now kowtow to a bunch of boring mutts
in a dog day-care centre?

Back at home, I decided not to send Winston
to this hysterical hen house ever again. And
anyway, you have to wonder: how good is
a dog-sitter who leaves her handbag in the
kennels? My enormous pride at my super-
nonconformist dog was very quickly superseded

by disillusionment mixed with doubt. Should I do something about Winston's turbulent attitude? Perhaps his unbridled energy needed professional direction, and then something really needed to be done about his jumping up. And perhaps if he could just look around when he joined a group of dogs to see if maybe there were other dogs there with more senior privileges whom it would be in his interest to respect?

My wife and I looked for a suitable dog trainer for Winston, and found one who had a "somewhat alternative dog training school." Now, I always have a healthy scepticism about anything that is marketed with dozy arrogance as being 'somewhat alternative,' because most of these things turn out to be as conventional as triangular cheese and pickle sandwiches. But because the guy made a really good impression on his website, we made an appointment with him.

The first lesson was encouraging: the dog trainer looked like a cross between Bob Dylan and a shepherd, and seemed to make contact with Winston on an almost telepathic level. He took our dog on the lead like a medium to whom you had to listen constantly. He put his head to one side, as if Winston could at any moment give a sign that we would then have to interpret. The dog man wrapped the lead delicately around one finger, as if he was leading a beautiful woman through the spa garden at Marienbad, but was, in fact, just leading the gherkin-headed Winston along a street in southeast Munich. He kept looking at the dog and instructed us to also keep looking at the dog all the time. "Can you see what he's doing?" he kept asking. We couldn't really answer that because Winston was just doing what he always did. Wandering about, sniffing about somewhere from time to time, stopping, pulling on the lead. But the dog man insisted on the marvel – the marvel that was Winston. "He is looking ..." he said. "... he is constantly looking at us. His head enables him to do this."

It's true that Winston possesses the anatomical capability of looking at people, even when he's standing with his back to them. His eyes are so cunningly situated in his gherkin-shaped head that he can see all around like a submarine periscope. "He is looking," repeated Alternative Man, as if the idea of dogs looking was something completely new. What he meant was that Winston was constantly looking at us. He was just waiting to receive commands from us, instructions that would open the door to the wonderful world of learning and understanding for him. The dog man praised everything about this dog that it is possible to: the shape of his head, his friendliness, and his curiosity. "He is looking. He is always looking," the dog man's enthusiasm knew no bounds. A woman with a pram came past and looked worriedly at Winston's gherkin head. "Did you see what he's doing?" asked the dog man. We shrugged. "He saw that the woman was afraid. And what does he do?" "He moves away. He sees that she is afraid and he steers away from her. He's a great dog."

We went away from this first dog training lesson feeling very proud, because it had confirmed for us that Winston was an unusually talented and sensitive dog. The dog man promised us that all of Winston's annoying problems – the jumping up, the pulling on the lead – could be overcome in ten lessons. It wouldn't take much to develop Winston into an easily manageable family dog. And please could we no longer patronize this dog day-care centre, which didn't understand anything about dogs? This would mean that we would have to leave Winston alone for several hours, only interrupted by a visit at midday when I took him out for a walk. "That can't be ideal, surely?" I asked. "Oh yes," contradicted the dog man, much to our relief. "Yes, that is ideal. Winston needs a little world in which to find his bearings. Other dogs are really miserable if they are left alone for long periods. But it's exactly the right thing for him."

Very good. Yes, very good that an expert confirmed to us that we had instinctively done everything right with Winston, although we had never had a dog before and therefore knew nothing about dealing with animals. However, there was still the matter of his attitude to the dog pack, so I asked the dog man what could be done about that.

"He won't take a subordinate role?" said the dog man. "That's right."

"It doesn't matter a damn."

To HELL WITH THE EXPERTS!

Lessons with the dog man continued and Winston always had much to work on when the three of us traipsed through the streets, with sudden stops here and there because the dog man had noticed yet another new fantastic and miraculous characteristic of our dog. "You see," said the dog man, "... he's a worker. He wants us to teach him something that he can then do."

Then came an evening when Winston was not in the mood for educational instruction, and did just about everything wrong that a dog of his age can do. He pulled on the lead, crapped at an inopportune moment, wouldn't take any direction, didn't want to cooperate with the man's gentle educational methods any point. The result was that the dog man called off the next lesson didn't respond to later requests for further lessons ...

The girls from the dog day-care centre couldn't get on with Winston, and the super dog man reached the end of his tether after five lessons. So

75

the training of Winston, the foundling dog, the
rejected Czech, was down to us. Since then,
at least I know that I can afford the opinions of
dog experts precious little weight. Dog trainers,
dog training schools, dog kennels – to hell with
them all! The only facility on which we have
thus far always been able to rely is a secluded
dog hotel in the south of Munich, where the
owners don't come up with any words of wisdom
or suggestions for interpretation with regard to
the essence of Winston, but instead just take
the dog as he is and look after him when we
go on holiday. In the pre–dog era, my wife and
I sometimes watched TV programmes about
obsessive dog-lovers in Germany. Of course,
there was always a part about the dogs being left
in so-called dog hotels. You saw tearful scenes
where the owners said goodbye to the animal;
an elderly couple disembarked onto a Spanish
island from their cruise ship and went straight to
an internet cafe, because there they could get
to the dog hotel's website and find out how their
little Fifi was getting on. We shook our heads at
the crazy behaviour that revealed a love for a
pet bordering on the unnatural. The first time we
left Winston in the dog hotel, we left a towel with
him, so that he could have the scent of home
if he felt miserable. We kept asking ourselves
if it was a good thing to do; if maybe the dog
would experience his delivery to dog paradise
as a betrayal, because he wouldn't know that it
was only temporary. A dog has no knowledge of
the word temporary. All his thinking takes place

in the here and now, and when we left, we were gone.

The holiday was great; Greece, hardly any tourists, good food and warm sea with small, well-behaved fish in it. But every time we met a dog (and that happens rather frequently in Greece) we were on the verge of ringing the dog hotel to check on Winston's emotional and physical wellbeing. Luckily, there was no internet cafe in the fishing village. When we returned, we learned that our dog had not sniffed the towel even once, but had made lots of canine friends and hadn't missed us for a single second. But we had missed him, thereby confirming we were right in the middle of the maelstrom into which this dog had drawn us, when we were unable to resist and had saved him from freezing to death. We responded to him with a sentimentality that the dog doesn't share at all; presumably, he doesn't think about us any more when we are away. It's possible that he completely forgets that we exist, whilst we see the fate of our dog in every Greek street mutt that comes into view and are moved by it. Is there really an actual policy of persecuting dogs in Greece? If there is, we're not going there any more. Out of protest.

Once I returned from a business trip and found Winston in a wretched state. He had been bitten during his stay in the kennels and had a huge gaping wound on his left foreleg. He squealed like a piglet when it was touched. It was already late evening and the dog minder drew a map for me showing the way to the

veterinary clinic. Of course, I got lost three
times, because this new scenario with Winston
made me nervous. This was all about illness and
the treatment thereof, things which, even as a
human, are better avoided. Eventually, I found
the clinic, which had a friendly atmosphere and
was staffed by young animal-lovers.

Winston had only a short wait to see the
vet. The wound was very deep and festering,
and the vet packed it with a dressing that she
had previously soaked in an antibiotic solution.
Winston was bandaged and now recognizable to
all as an injured dog. To top it off – and I mean
this literally – he had a plastic funnel placed
around his neck which was to stop him from
gnawing off the carefully wrapped bandage.
He was not very happy about this arrangement
because it severely restricted his movement
and also made him look rather silly. Dogs
clearly pick up on embarrassing situations and
feel something similar to shame, but why, for
goodness sake, doesn't the dog feel embarrassed
about the things that are embarrassing for me?
Why is he not ashamed about jumping up at
people or pulling on the lead like a yob when he
is supposed to be walking nicely? Why doesn't
he blush when he's just peed on the bathroom
floor because he can't be bothered to go outside?

The injury to Winston's paw just didn't
want to heal. We showed it to various vets, and
every time conventional treatment of ointment
and antibiotics was prescribed. Eventually, an
unusually clever vet thought of x-raying the

 paw, which revealed a piece of
tooth – belonging to the dog who
had bitten Winston – buried deep
in the tissue. An operation was
necessary, and so, at the age
of a year, Winston already had
to go under the scalpel, happily,
wielded by a well-trained surgeon who
completely resolved the problem with the paw.
It was like a victory on the battlefield, when the
bandy-legged, gherkin-headed dog stumbled
along the clinic hallway after the operation,
utterly dazed by the anaesthetic, but completely
free of pain and inflammation. I still have the
tooth fragment belonging to his attacker, and
keep it in a narrow plastic tube like a religious
relic.

This was only one chapter in the medical
history of the dog, which has already cost us
a small fortune. The money we have spent on
medication, x-rays, injections, and treatments
would have quite easily covered a three-
week holiday on the Cote d'Azur. The dog
eats everything, including plastic bags and
the choicest parts of his leather collar. One
morning I found a small piece of it in some vomit
that he had kindly left on the tiled bathroom
floor rather than on the carpet. Off to the vet
– again. X-ray – again. They couldn't rule out
an intestinal obstruction, according to the vet, a
serious young woman who had a great respect
for animals, which I liked. She said that they
could, of course, just treat the symptoms, but

if we wanted to be on the safe side an x-ray examination would be necessary, and this could cost two hundred euros. Just for a moment I thought: that's not really my dog; some other people abandoned him; I can't always have to keep paying, surely? Maybe the state should pay the two hundred euros: as I had taken on the care of the dog instead it being left to the relevant authorities, the city of Munich should cover the incidental expenses.

If Winston had to have an operation now because of the plastic bags he had eaten, I would definitely have to ask the bank for an overdraft. However, the results of the x-ray gave the all-clear: there was no intestinal obstruction, the dog did not need to stay in the clinic, but instead just had to eat a special and extremely expensive diet food for a few days – which he didn't like. The vet gave me the bill first and then a large plastic bag full of filled syringes, drops, antibiotics and packets of special, easily digestible dog food. When I got home after three hours, I drank a whole bottle of white wine in half an hour, I felt that bad. I would spend all my savings for the dog, if it came to it. I used to watch TV reports on high-tech veterinary medicine with astonishment, which showed, in unbelievably well-equipped operating rooms, an old tomcat undergoing

open-heart surgery, German Shepherds receiving
artificial hips, and even hamsters having tumours
removed. Going to so much expense and trouble
for an animal? I wouldn't even think of asking
this question any more these days. Today, if
Winston was seriously ill, I would fly to the USA if
designated specialists there could save my dog.
But why? In gratitude for the way he restricts my
life, ruins our apartment and shreds my nerves
like the plastic carrier bags that end up in his
jaws?

What on earth compels us to love our dogs
so much ...?

WE DISCOVER COMMON ENEMIES

There are dog owners who take their animals everywhere with them. They can't go to a beer garden, on an outing, not even on their summer holidays without the dog. For the dog, these journeys, both long and short, are, of course, always very pleasant; but for me, a holiday represents the only opportunity to completely get away from everything that is difficult and stressful – and the dog belongs unequivocally in this category.

Because the tourist industry is aware of this dilemma, it has invented lots of clever solutions. For example, there are dog hotels where master, mistress and little doggy can all stay under one roof, but be looked after separately. The dog owners can go to the lavender grotto or be sprinkled with Ayurvedic gubbins, whilst the dogs are looked after by qualified dog minders. Indeed, the dogs don't just enjoy walks in the Alps or on the mudflats, but also have spa treatments – such as Kneipp paddling and the like. There are even – and now we are again entering the great border zone between love and madness – cultural city tours for dogs. This service is aimed at animals like the amazing mongrel bitch from the English Garden, who was capable of sniffing out the cultural landscape of Italy in an enthusiastic yet discerning manner. Small groups of people and dogs really do get together in order to discover the great cultural heritage of Riga, Vienna, Regensburg, and Prague.

In Prague, incidentally, a commemorative plaque for the author Bohumil Hrabel was fixed to the wall at just the right height for dogs to pee on it, as per his express wish. Of course, we have also taken Winston on some trips, because you can't leave a dog alone for eight hours in an apartment. Winston likes – and this is really lucky and saves us a lot of trouble – indeed, he loves, going in the car. At the beginning he was allowed to travel in the front passenger footwell. After a brief period of euphoria during which he licked the passenger copiously and jumped all over them, he relaxed and went to sleep. The journeys were therefore always very pleasant and Winston never gave us any cause to complain about him in this respect.

Once, we visited the little place Marktl am Inn, primarily known for being the birthplace of the current Pope. As we stood outside the house where Joseph Ratzinger was born, a jeep stopped and out jumped a long-haired young man, who began extolling the virtues of our dog's breed and appearance in a strong, Lower Bavarian accent. He told us that he had had a dog just like this for many years and was so

keen on this breed that he always had to stop
whenever one crossed his path. I thanked him
and tried to rein in Winston's enthusiasm with the
lead.

However, not everyone is pleased to make
Winston's acquaintance whilst engaged in leisure
activities, particularly if his manner is somewhat
unfriendly. I took him on a fairly long trip to a
small and also very unattractive holiday resort
in the Tyrol. The only attraction as far as I
could see was a forest in which you could walk
without meeting the usual groups of walkers
and families. A little stream was fed by water
from a narrow river, and between the two was
a meadow in which I set Winston free to do his
rabbit-like jumps. Suddenly, he ran a few paces
towards the path, without prior consultation with
me. He positioned himself in all his hulking,
muscular glory at the edge of the path, and
began to issue a series of short, sharp barks that
froze the blood in your veins. The Nordic walker
who was approaching must have experienced
this sensation as soon as he saw Winston, as
he stood as if paralysed in front of the barking
dog, who had obviously been scared by the
noise made by the silly Nordic walking sticks,
which was why he had begun barking. I told off
Winston firmly, put him on the lead and punished
him with a slap on his behind, which he accepted
whilst remaining unconcerned and having learnt
nothing. The man, by contrast, was extremely
indignant and lectured me for several minutes
about how he couldn't stand being told by dog

owners that their animals were harmless; he had
already been bitten by two supposedly lovable
dogs and he demanded that I put my dog on the
lead when I was walking him on public paths. To
put it bluntly, the man was right on every score,
which was precisely why I despised him. I didn't
like his self-righteousness and I didn't like his
silly appearance. At the same time, I discovered
a new common interest with Winston, who
obviously disliked Nordic walkers as much as I
did. This silly person hadn't just scared my dog,
but presumably on his long and ludicrous march
had scared away hordes of wild animals, deer,
weasels, and goodness knows what else. He
was the troublemaker in this peaceful Tyrolean
landscape, not Winston. Nordic walkers – and
I have to explain this in order to flesh out the
image of this bogeyman – belong to that group
of people who accept all the rubbish peddled by
fitness gurus. They would put pigs' bladders on
their heads and hop through the mountains on
one leg if a wellness coach told them that this
would keep their circulation and digestive system
in good shape. Nordic walkers are big, ridiculous
weirdos who strut around, preposterously proud
of themselves, completely unaware of their
surroundings. Winston, who is closer to nature
than civilization, sensed this and his loud barking
was his denouncement of it. I would also go so
far as to say that if I had been the dog in this
situation, I would have bitten a hole in the man's
arse as big as a barn door. The man moved
on after I had made it clear to him where he

could stick his lectures, and I called him a few choice things under my breath afterwards. I gave Winston a biscuit bone as a reward. The dog had demonstrated his good taste and a completely uncompromising ability to judge character.

Nevertheless, it is still really unpleasant when your dog appears to strangers to be a fearful monster, because you really want to have your own peaceable nature typified by your dog. Patricia B McConnell, an American zoologist, wrote an astonishingly wise book about dogs. It is called *The other end of the leash* and contains the following sensible statement: "We can't live together with animals which have the equivalent of carpet knives in their mouths without having some problems from time to time." As, for example, when the dog runs up to a walker who doesn't have a relaxed attitude to dogs, and who looks extremely afraid when confronted by a Bull Terrier running towards him doing bunny hops. What should you say to the man? The phrase "He won't do anything, he just wants to play," has been parodied too often for an intelligent person to want to say it any more. And yet, in general it is entirely accurate and the only alternative. Or should you shout every time: "Don't be afraid, my dog aims to astonish you in the next few minutes with his three-stage entertainment programme; he will place his forepaws in your crotch region, lick your hands with his heavy, wet tongue and then check your jacket pockets for food."? Hmmm, maybe not ...

Most dog owners know this unsavoury canine

habit well enough and put up with it with a smile.
Interestingly, as a dog owner you tend to be out
and about mostly in areas where almost all other
people are out and about with dogs. Or no other
people – as far as you can see.

There is a lovely big meadow near
Holzhausen by Lake Starnberg, a landscape
of gently rolling mounds, a slight slope which
causes you to walk a little more quickly, and fruit
trees, which point to there once having been an
estate with a luxuriant garden here. When the
weather is good, there is the beautiful panorama
of the Wendelstein rising up behind the little
green onion-domed church, the Friedhofskapelle
in Holzhausen. I go to this meadow with
Winston when I want him to run himself
systematically and directly into a virtual
stupor. I throw a ball down the slope
and he races after it as if he has to
defuse seven anti-tank mines in the
next two seconds, and comes running
back to me, proudly holding the yellow tennis
ball in his mouth.

Of course, officially he should hand over
the ball immediately, but he doesn't do that. He
sees the ball as prey, which belongs exclusively
to him, but which he will perhaps let go of if
something more interesting appears. When
Winston has the yellow tennis ball in his mouth,
he has two desires in him fighting for supremacy:
on the one hand, he would like to keep the ball
in his mouth and chew on it; on the other hand,
he would really like it if the ball could be thrown

very hard for him so that he can race after it like
the devil after poor, lost souls.

Incidentally, the view from this meadow is
indescribable. The Wendelstein is visible not
just when the weather is good, but you can also
make out its silhouette on a cloudy and misty
day. Behind the hill lies Lake Starnberg and, at
moments like these, I am again moved to recall
the mongrel bitch in the English Garden, who
would perhaps show suitable appreciation of
the landscape and would agree with her master
when he claimed that this scenery – with its
gentle hills – had something Tuscan about it.
When I turn around, I see that Winston is rolling
in the grass with all four paws pointing at the
beautiful blue sky. When he comes running up
to me, I smell the strong stench of the chemical-
saturated liquid manure in which he has just
wallowed. This meadow is, of course, also
part of untamed nature and therefore has in it
animals that prey on other animals in order to
make it through the year well-fed and healthy.
At the edge of the maize field I once found the
remains of a dismembered rabbit, that the hunter
– which I assume to have been a fox – had strewn
wildly around the meadow. The pelt had been
completely removed and the backbone exposed;
the head had, presumably, been dragged
elsewhere. Just one rabbit leg remain untouched,
left in the grass to rot. Obviously, Winston could
not overlook this delicious snack. As he went to
put his muzzle near the wet part of the corpse,
I was able to stop him from sampling the fur

with a sharp 'No,' but he still managed to get hold of the revolting leg. I have never had to do anything more nauseating than pull this sickly-sweet-smelling, partially rotted rabbit leg out of the dog's jaws, although, unfortunately, achieved only a partial victory, as Winston crunched down on the lower part of the rabbit's leg with his powerful teeth – an action which made a gruesome sound.

Once, we were trudging, tired and played out, along the rutted path on the way back from the idyllic dog meadow when a van, in which was an elderly man, a young man and a dog, came bumping towards us. When they had passed us, the van stopped, a sliding door opened and the dog, a young dalmatian, jumped out at Winston and barked at him loudly so that Winston jumped to the side in surprise. Even as he was jumping, Winston must have seen the open van door, perhaps also already guessing that there was something inside that he might like. In a flash, my dog had jumped into the van and immediately he was in there began to lick the young man's face. After ensuring that his salt needs had been met, Winston turned his attention to the back seat on which there was a box of biscuits which he obviously intended to suck up with his long nose.

Unfortunately, I didn't get to the scene to pull the dog out of the van until this theft was already well under way. I apologized profusely but my apologies were waved away with the words: "When all is said and done, we all just want to have a bit of fun." Evidently, dyed-in-the-wool dog lovers find it pleasant when a dog completely ignores all the rules pertaining to custom and decency and makes as big an exhibition of himself as he can. Winston was then given the biscuits that he had been after but had not managed to get to. Out of annoyance at the insanity of my dog, I later petulantly threw the biscuits into the furrows of the field.

Something similar had happened a couple of months previously in the area near the German/Austrian border in the little town of Burghausen. I had walked Winston on the lead through the stone monuments to the feudal culture around there, but without being able to achieve any particular educational effect. He was well-behaved and keeping a low profile, so I let him off the lead to let him at least have a sniff around the area. Just at the exact moment that I set him free, a fiendishly good smell must have reached Winston's nose, because he suddenly took off at breakneck speed. I ran behind him and arrived just in time to see Winston making for a car belonging to two women who were just feeding their refined little poodle. One of the women threw Winston a piece of sausage to make him go away. Once again, I apologized profusely, mightily relieved that nothing else had happened.

These kinds of things are obviously what happens when you are out and about with a dog. Excursions with Winston are like transporting a prisoner in as much as the delinquent can escape at any moment and take hostages.

Does He Go in the Water too?

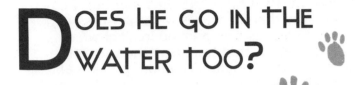

Many dogs like nothing better on hot summer days than to jump into a lake or a stream and enjoy a quiet swim up and down. "Does your dog go in the water too?" is the question that dog owners pose to sound out the social competence of a strange dog.

Winston has a somewhat ambivalent relationship to water. He senses – that is to say, experience has taught him – that water has a very pleasantly refreshing effect on his body, but he is afraid of the unpredictable power of the element, so he never goes out of his depth in streams and rivers, instead staying where his paws can touch the bottom. Once, I took Winston to a lake as he needed to see the natural wonder of an alpine lake and find out how to deal with it. At the shoreline, the dog discovered a phenomenon that initially repelled or scared him: waves. A fresh gust of wind blew over the water and ruffled it gently so that little white crested waves kept swimming to the shore and broke there. Winston ran away from them every time, his gaze fixed on the strange thing that obviously wanted to catch him and, who knows, mistreat him. After half an hour, he had recognized that the waves were harmless and remembered his own hunting instinct which enabled him to start to pursue the waves instead. His enthusiasm and anticipation of being able to catch a big one drove him so far into the lake that he could no longer stand, and there were also no more breaking waves to enjoy. It took him quite a while to notice that he was swimming, but when he did, he got a terrible shock and paddled back to the bank and solid ground under his paws. Winston stood there, shivering pointedly. The water had offended him: he wanted to go.

A dog has reached an extremely high level of civilization when he manages to go swimming with his master or mistress. After all, every form of life originally came from the water, and when dog and man are splashing around together in the primeval soup, another big piece of the foreignness between them dissolves. I was very envious when I read that chapter in Konrad Lorenz's book *Man meets Dog*, in which he describes how he swims along a really broad tributary of the Danube with his dog, Susi. At first, according to Lorenz, Susi keeps looking back towards the bank they started from, because she is frightened of the long distance. But then she develops such a deep trust in her master's ability to find his way that she goes along with it. Eventually, they come to a sandbank where Susi can chase sticks and generally indulge her play instincts. They walk

back and clever Susi keeps jumping into the water – despite her recent long swim – to hunt frogs.

Sometimes, I think that dogs primarily go into the water for the sake of their owner. A swimming dog makes a sporty and intelligent impression – he seems independent and self-reliant. Dogs should always be sporty; the modern person's great desire for fitness, physical equilibrium, wellness and health is transferred in its entirety to their dog, and that begins, as with everything health-related, with nutrition. Anyone who favours Mediterranean cuisine for their family will never start cooking without cold-pressed olive oil, and so only cold-pressed food makes its way into the dog's bowl: duck and menhaden herring, cold-pressed, lamb and beef with brown rice and wheat germ oil – holistic cuisine for dogs. A dog with the correct lifestyle appreciates cold-pressed cooking and afterwards manages a couple of refined laps in a naturally pure, cold-pressed lake. All the therapeutic stuff with which people deflect their fear of illness and death is also directed at dogs. If I fed Winston with one hundred per cent organic food, I would have a good, perhaps even politically correct feeling, but I would be closing my eyes to the fact that this dog likes to supplement his own diet. If the wind blows a plastic bag in front of his nose, Winston will eat this with an expression of culinary comprehension, regardless of whether or not the plastic bag is cold-pressed. The plastic bag will line his colon like a delicate black membrane and sound out the prospects for the next intestinal obstruction. Winston also eats hard plastic and attempts to split drinks bottles with his teeth into small bite-sized morsels. He does not shrink from tasting goat crap if he chances on it in a field – although perhaps this completes the cycle of organic food, depending on your point of view and whether the goat has previously eaten something cold-pressed. However, the dog's health is not only regulated by his absurdly varied diet; exercise is the magic word.

I have always felt a mixture of admiration and pity for those dogs who have to go jogging with their owners. They run alongside their sweating owners like bodyguards, looking longingly at the flying red frisbees and yellow tennis balls arcing alluringly through the air – sadly out of reach. They would like to catch the disc or ball in their mouth, but they are forced to jog, just as other, similarly conditioned dogs have to run beside bicycles. I have always felt it to be a terrible tribulation for a dog when he has to join in with his owner's leisure activities. Despite this, I still tried it once with Winston, who ran next to me on his lead for three quarters of an hour and did the whole fitness thing somewhat reluctantly but obediently. It didn't occur to Winston until we were on our way back that disobedience is actually one of his specialities, whereupon he threw himself down in the grass and didn't get up for a good long time before trotting back to the car at a civilized tempo.

There is one form of exercise that is much more idiotic than rushing around jogging tracks: teaching dogs tricks. Once, when buying food for Winston, I visited a pet shop in Starnberg and met a woman at the till who was getting her Scottish Terrier to perform like a circus animal. The dog stood on his hind legs like a wobbly little man, which is a performance that degrades the dog and makes it look ridiculous. Anyway, the dog's owner told the cashier that her dog could do even more tricks, but she didn't have enough time at that point to get him to demonstrate all of them. Thank God for that. Aside from the fact that it would be completely pointless to introduce Winston to the world of active acrobatics, there's one thing I have to say: people who train their dogs to perform ridiculous tricks belong in the circus ring, in therapy or in some other kind of funny institution, but not out on the street. What do you gain from a dog who is walking on two legs? What use to me is a canine who balances a table tennis ball on his nose? None at all.

One of my favourite stories about a dog was written by B W – not Raymond – Chandler. A married couple lives with their dog in a town where it has recently become compulsory for dogs to wear a muzzle. The dog always skilfully manages to avoid the muzzle until finally a policeman complains. The dog, who is clever and well-trained, offers the policeman a dollar bill and its owners are then immediately awarded a steep fine on the grounds of bribery. The narrator concludes his account with the sentence: "I want a stupid dog." That's what I want too.

Or maybe not?

THE DOG IN WORLD LITERATURE

Sometimes Winston doesn't seem to be there at all; that is to say, obviously I know that he must be there because he can't leave the apartment by himself, and all of the windows and doors are shut. Nevertheless, I have to look for him, especially since he doesn't answer when he is called. It is only his quiet, breathy snoring that will betray him at some point and he is discovered in the wardrobe, nestled between pillows and eiderdowns. He is keeping quiet because he doesn't want to give up this comfortable spot under any circumstances, in the same way as he does not want to stop rearranging the sofa cushions so that they form a little hollow with just the right contours for his gherkin-shaped head. And if he has been particularly skilful, part of his short, tri-coloured body will fit into the cavity and then it may be a while before I find him. When he is lying there sleeping, I notice how all my nerves relax, because I know that for the next hour he's not going to eat or chew anything he shouldn't; that he's not going to bark or growl, and will not want to eat or have a pee; that he's just closed his eyes to little black slits and has gone to sleep. The dog is switched to standby, and I can devote myself to pleasant activities – such as reading books about dogs, for example.

I don't mean all that advisory literature which I have referred to already and which frequently borders on the insane, but instead the many wonderful literary stories written about dogs and their masters. For example, James Thurber's* tale of a dog who bit everybody, and whose mistress found an excuse for every bite. Or, by the same author, the story of Rex the Bull Terrier, who dragged furniture out of old houses and at the end drops down dead in front of his master – who has just arrived home – because he was injured in an unfair fight with some other dogs. And not forgetting P G Wodehouse's short story** in which a dog tells how he hunts down a burglar just because of his faithful nature and good training – even though he received that courtesy of the very same burglar! And then, of course, there is Thomas Mann's *Man and Dog: an Idyll*, the story of Bauschan, the Pointer, who lived as a bag of bones on a farmstead in Bad Tolz until he was adopted into the well-off Mann family and there rose, as it were, to the position of four-legged private secretary to the author.

*James Thurber: *Snapshot of a dog* (Rex the Bull Terrier) and *The dog that bit people*, in James Thurber's *Writings and Drawings*.
**P G Wodehouse: *The Mixer*, in P G Wodehouse's *The Man with Two Left Feet and other stories*.

I still do not understand how Thomas Mann managed to leave the poor dog locked in the horrendous cage of the Institute for Veterinary Medicine in Munich for two weeks, supervised by a complete idiot of a keeper. Of course, Bauschan just kept getting thinner and sadder and Mann must have seen that. And why did a prospective Nobel prizewinner allow himself to be dictated to by a mangy animal keeper about how long he should leave his dog mouldering in this horrible mess? It goes without saying that Bauschan became estranged from his master in the weeks following this episode. He couldn't do anything else if he wanted to retain what remained of his dignity as a dog. This episode also demonstrates how far the Institute of Veterinary Medicine has come since then. These days, dogs receive more comprehensive treatment than people did in the era when Thomas Mann wrote his dog tale.

What else don't I like about Thomas Mann's short story? The authoritarian training regime, for one thing. He beats the Pointer with a strap or a stick – this is completely reactionary and can only be in any way forgiven because the author produced a very nice turn of phrase to communicate the fact that Bauschan crapped in his house: "He defiled my study."

The great thing about all of these texts, and the many other stories by other famous dog owners like Kipling, Twain and Herriot, is that they all had similar problems with their Bauschans, Rexes and Jupiters to the ones I have with Winston. Then there is also the faction comprised of literary dog haters, who actually set to work in a much more sophisticated way. It is always said of Kurt Tucholsky that he couldn't stand dogs. We have to clear up this prejudice once and for all, because Tucholsky also wrote a sentence that belongs in the treasury of clever dog sayings: "No, I do not hate the dog. But instead a certain type of person who treats the dog like a brigade commander treats his unit and who potters about with him because he's German."

At this point, we must once again turn our attention to masters and perhaps even especially to mistresses, although I must point out that, in general, women are much braver and less mistrustful in their dealings with dogs than are men. But it was still two fairly weird old bags who recently got me into a situation – which I truly didn't realise how absurd this was until it was over.

Everyone who has anything to do with dogs knows that a game of ball is a great and serious concern for every canine. If Winston gets possession of another dog's ball, he doesn't like to give it up without a fight, and I have already explained this eccentricity of his in detail. There is a certain logic in this, because dogs are prey animals, and why shouldn't a nice, shiny ball be a good prey object when there is no mole or squirrel around at that precise moment? In any case, these two – and I must be blunt here – hags were watching increasingly grumpily as

Winston got hold of their ball, which had a silly rope attached to it and which the ladies therefore believed to be a special ball, and wouldn't give it back. I noticed the hags getting impatient because their ball was lost. They seemed to be more attached to the ball than to their own constantly growling and yapping mutt, which they shouted at incessantly. I was harangued by this irritating, caustic and completely hysterical pair and was obliged to get the silly ball away from Winston.

Of course, I didn't succeed. Every time I got within reach of Winston, he skilfully changed direction and ended up a couple of metres further away with his prey in his mouth. He ran round on the grass in big circles because the ball made him so happy, and the happier the ball made him, the unhappier the hags became until one of them tried to pull the ball out of Winston's mouth, at the same time shouting at the dog just as she presumably usually shouted at her husband. I watched and abandoned any attempt to explain to the red-hennaed fury that she would get no response whatsoever from yelling at the dog. The woman wanted the ball; it was her ball. Hers. It frightened me to realise that there are dog owners whose values exactly match those of their dogs.

Of course, the episode with the henna hags doesn't lend itself one hundred per cent to substantiating the Tucholsky statement about the implementation of dogs as a – watch out, I'm laying it on extra-thick here – semi-fascist tool of battle. The following story works better in that respect: I once had to visit Sardinia and was staying with a group of journalists in a country house belonging to someone who had previously fought in what used to be known as the Belgian Congo. The man was titled and in his younger days had been in the Foreign Legion, and therefore was undoubtedly one of those men who have sophisticated methods of killing silently. A melancholy killer; a master of destruction – and I'm really only exaggerating a little bit.

Anyway, this man owned two enormous Rottweilers, which barked at anyone who came within fifty metres of the house. I felt it sensible to stay as far away as possible from the Belgian Congo fighter and his canine vassals, and followed the narrow path that led directly from his enviably beautiful property to the white, sandy beach, a pretty, sandy walkway through tall sea grass. When I arrived at the beach, I looked back and admired the attractive curve of the little track, just like those in the South Sea Islands stories by Somerset Maugham, and I waited in the silence for an elegant young woman in a dragonfly costume to come sweeping down from the villa to the beach to invite me for sophisticated cold drinks. However, what was actually making its way towards me was equally as likely to put me into a persistent vegetative state, though not quite as pleasantly. Racing down the narrow path like a raiding party came the two Rottweilers, and from their gait and the look in their eyes, I could tell that it was not a spontaneous dip in the sea they were after, but more likely a bloodbath. They had it in for me but I didn't yet know how and to what extent. I stood still; indeed, I was so shocked that I couldn't do anything else other than stand still and take things – or in fact, dogs – as they came. The sight of the big, incredibly fast dogs was like an image of mercilessly disappearing time. Ten, twelve seconds and they would be down here to end my uneventful life on an unspectacular beach in southern Sardinia.

With bated breath I waited. The two marauding canines stopped directly before me and looked; first at me, and then at my shoes. Then at me again. This continued for about a minute; obviously, the dogs could not decide whether to attack me or go away, so I tried taking a step with my right foot. Immediately the duo threw themselves on my shoe and pulled on my shoelaces. I stood still and stiff again and they let go. I tried another step and again the huge animals threw themselves on my shoes. Of course they were playing, really enjoying pulling on my shoelaces, and had come all the way from the villa to the beach just for this. I don't know how long I stood there. fearful of taking a single step, but, at some point, the Congo fighter whistled from his terrace and suddenly the Rottweilers left me, the two huge black barrels of muscle, bone and teeth sending up clouds of sand as they bounded back to their lord and master.

WINSTON ...

Shortly after I learned from a colleague who was also staying in the Congo fighter's house that he had had a similar experience with the pair the previous evening when he had forgotten his room key and looked for an alternative way of entry. Initially, he was overjoyed to note that the window of his room was open and so began to climb in like a burglar. Less than ten seconds later, at least one of the demonic duo had realised what was going on, and a raiding party was immediately set in motion. One of the leaping dogs got extremely close to the window which my colleague had hurriedly wriggled through and shut from the inside.

The dogs would have had such a nice life if they had just lain every day in the Sardinian sun, opening a heavy eyelid from time to time to peer at the horizon. Instead, they had to constantly symbolise their owner's profession, guarding, barking, attacking and, if necessary, silently killing – which each of them could have managed in the twinkling of an eye.

I WILL CHANGE

Sometimes I think it's completely pointless waiting for the dog to adapt to us; for him to betray his nature and accept our way of life. For him one day to say, okay, these people are delicate creatures committed to non-aggressive and communicative principles, who don't cause me many problems, and want to integrate me into their benignly liberal coexistence. Perhaps I should gradually give up my dominant behaviour and simply submit, out of pure philanthropy.

But the truth is this: the dog will always exploit our weaknesses and good nature and use them to further his own interests, and we can do nothing about this because the dog is never, ever going to change. And so *we* have to change; get tough or, even better, as aloof as those dog owners who only speak to their animals when absolutely necessary and communicate everything else through gestures and beatings. Severe and pitiless are these individuals, perhaps spiced with a dash of very unpleasant unscrupulousness, like the Belgian Congo fighter, whose dogs only responded to whistles. The

WINSTON ...

Belgian never spoke to the animals. He sat on his terrace, knocking back Belgian beer and the dogs lay at his feet – always alert, always ready to receive a silent, dictatorial sign from their lord and master, so that they could immediately go and rip up some shoelaces or something bigger.

Hardly any other dog is as obedient as the one belonging to the chav who goes to the dog walking area dressed in tracksuit trousers and vest, and throws his German Shepherd a couple of grim, one-syllable commands. All the chatter that a dog is subject to, day in, day out, in dog-friendly families, drives the animal crazy because it's unnatural for him. A dog doesn't talk himself, but is blabbered at the whole day long. Sometimes I dream of being a really aloof dog owner, who calls his mutt with a whistle and is rewarded with nothing other than obedience and subservience. At some point late in the afternoon – when it suits me, me, and not the dog! – I would put on my padded anorak and call the dog to my side with a shrill whistle. And then we would go to the dog park, where the dog would, of course, first assume a submissive position in response to a click of my fingers, a second click allowing him to get up and rush off to play with the other dogs and express the natural aggression which he has to suppress in my presence. I would throw a few choice insults at anyone who was scared and called out to me that I should just put my dog on the lead. Or I would give the dog a curt order to sort out the passerby on his terms.

And I wouldn't talk to other dog owners any more. No more tedious exchanges, no more amiable comparisons of animals: "Yes, my dog is exactly the same: once he's got hold of the ball he doesn't want to give it up." Oh no, there wouldn't be any more of that for me. The dog wouldn't even dare take a ball in his mouth without first receiving a wordless, gestured command from me, nor any longer return balls belonging to other dogs, because I would see that as a sign of weakness, which is prohibited among dog chavs. Would I teach the dog to snap? Possibly, yes, although dog chavs wouldn't like to be pestered, but just lurk as a silent, dull presence in the half-shadows. My interpersonal contact would also be limited to like-minded people, blokes from the dog walking area, who would wear anoraks with shoulder pads like me and be taciturn. Of course, the dogs would also have virtually nothing to do with each other, aligning themselves with their masters' disinclination to communicate and lead a strange, solitary life. As a chav, of course, I would have to give up my current behaviour of favouring people like me. But how relaxed the afternoons at the dog walking area would be if we all squatted silently in front of our crates of beer and the dogs lay in front of us in the dust like slaughtered buffalos, an extraordinary and archaic world, in which dogs and people interacted on exactly the same level, where peace reigned and a great silence connected owner and dog forever ...

THAT IS HIS CHARACTER

We have had Winston for more than two years now, and if I wanted to put a positive spin on it, I would say that he has enriched our life. For example, he ensures that we don't spend the whole day at home, reading, listening to music or wasting our time with various other useless activities, and schedules our life to such an extent that we are not just obliged to see our own pleasantly manageable circle of acquaintances, but also have to meet new people every day who explain the world to us – the dog's world, of course. Winston has thought out a sensible, healthy lifeplan for us; he structures our days cleverly and is very farsighted, and the interesting and novel thing is that these days now start at seven o'clock in the morning.

They also start at this time when it is still dark outside, because the glorious summer has given way to miserable autumn and the street lights illuminate the big raindrops that plop into the already large puddles like fat frogs. At this time, I have to walk with the dog through wet fields, for which I have bought myself wellington boots especially – my first since childhood. I wear

108

what I always detested when I saw other people wearing it – practical functional clothing, that is as water repellent as it is ugly. The dog has therefore also managed to rid me of the majority of my aesthetic standards. I am now moving in the same circles as the indestructible dog mummies, who are wearing similar clothes and who are not dissuaded by either wind or weather from romping through the fields with their darlings. When Winston jumps up at these mummies, he is applauded, which makes me relieved but also makes my battle to stop his dreadful jumping up all the harder. Unfortunately, even at this depressingly early hour, there are people already dressed for the office who are taking their well-behaved dogs for a quick walk in the field. This then, is their opportunity to make the acquaintance of my badly behaved dog, who jumps up on their white trousers and leaves his unique paw prints all over them. It's his visiting card – introducing Winston; always cheerful and opposing every attempt at training with natural scepticism.

Because I don't enjoy these kinds of encounters much, I try to take Winston to lonelier areas of the fields, in which he can rush around, catch balls and maybe bring them back, or drag huge branches around like a forestry worker. The dog slaves away with these branches like crazy, driving them through the grass like snowploughs. Sometimes, I am aware of a walkway opening up through the grass, but can't actually see Winston.

The dog park is dominated by an old, well-grown tree, an oak, I think. For decades, the function of this tree was, presumably, to provide shade in summer, and perhaps just to be a nice tree. These days, the tree is a sort of noticeboard, where you can read announcements by the Castle and Lake Management Authority, which also manages the English Garden, interspersed with advertisements for dog-sitting or dog-training services. When I recently told my wife about a notice written on a piece of paper with a tear-off fringe of telephone numbers along the bottom, she immediately snapped a very sharp, stern "No." God knows, I had not intended to ring up and add to our household the "little Greek, four month old, animal refuge orphan, looking for a family who will love him very much."

News generally spreads around the dog park even without the use of the tree. Winston's story is common knowledge here; anyone who doesn't know is soon filled in on the details of the story of my dog. That Winston loves jumping up at people is also common knowledge, and regarded by some as a lovable quirk, but by others as a disgraceful habit. From time to time in the latter camp there are elderly ladies with white pudding bowl haircuts who march in their imitation Gucci coats over the meadows of the dog park and nearly wet themselves when a dog jumps up at them. Conversely, I learn a fair bit about bitches

on heat, from whom I have to protect Winston,
as well as the affinity that my dog has with a
certain type of Irish Terrier.

"She's on heat," a young woman calls out to
me in place of a greeting.

"It doesn't matter, he's castrated!" I call
back.

I could never have imagined that I would ever
have this sort of conversation. Indeed, likewise I
have never imagined that I would arrange for an
animal to be castrated. Many experts advised us
to do this because it would curb the dog's natural
aggression and reduce his excitability. Winston
was never aggressive, and the other effect,
unfortunately, never kicked in. Perhaps he would
also chase after every possible bitch if he wasn't
castrated – I have no idea. Others responded
to my announcement that I was going to have
Winston's testicles removed with gentle rebukes.
However, none of these people could really
justify their doubts about whether castration
was the appropriate measure to take. After all,
a dog really doesn't care if he has testes or not.
If someone tried to take Winston's bone off him
that would upset him much more.

I haven't yet completed my study of the
laws of the dog park, but I presume that many
things are based on compromises with the
park management. In the happy time, when I
didn't have a dog, there must have been fierce
discussions about dogs having to be a lead,
and that kind of thing. Consequently, fans of
freedom of movement founded the Human

and Dog Forum (Forum Mensch und Hund), which, as indicated by the name, champions an agreeable environment for both people and dogs. This includes ensuring that every pile of crap is removed immediately by the dog owner, regardless of whether this is lying in the company of thousands of sheep droppings, which the dog is keen to eat as many of as possible. It's certainly disgusting, but the truth is sometimes harsh in the canine world. The fact that sheep have the privilege of grazing in the English Garden is felt by many dog owners to be unjust, because the sheep in their innocence and vulnerability – as already symbolized by their snow white wool – constitute a sharp contrast to the boisterous dogs. It seems that the sheep is always in the right, because it is weak and defenceless. The whole thing has a bit of a whiff of the Old Testament about it. Incidentally, recently two German Shepherds got in amongst the herd of sheep and injured some animals, one very severely, and so the subject of animals having to be on a lead is back on the political agenda, but can you really expect sheep to graze on a lead ...? "We ensure that our dogs behave properly, but the shepherds let their animals crap everywhere. And in addition to this, the ancient trees are being chopped down," say those dog owners who want to play off sheep and dog.

Many dog owners also exhibit great mistrust

of cyclists, whose allegedly reckless riding
endangers the dogs, even if they are on the lead.
Time and again, there are small- to medium-
sized disputes when cyclists and dogs collide,
whether because the cyclist wasn't paying
attention to the dog or whether – and this is
where it gets dramatic – because the dog ran
barking after the cyclist and hunted down him
or her. I have witnessed this same phenomenon
in relation to dogs and joggers. Dogs who chase
joggers are seen as ready for violent intervention,
which at first sight is not reasonable, because
why should a creature that is running after
another want to kill it? I believe that in at least
one respect I have managed to do the right thing
with Winston's training: I don't take him jogging
and I also steer well clear of cycle rides as these
are unpleasant for the dog, because a dog that
is trained to joggers and bikes will of course
chase after them – it's all to do with training and
I understand a whole lot about this, when all is
said and done.

Many dog owners feel disadvantaged
because they don't get a reward for keeping
their dogs under control. All the other people
and sheep can do what they want and only
dogs have to be disciplined. This is why they
often tend to come out with desperate general
eco-criticism. Everything is allowed to slide into
degeneracy, the profiteers insult nature, but
the dogs still have to do everything correctly. I
don't share this attitude of cultural pessimism,
but with Winston take the opposite tack of using

the irresistible range of services offered by the wilderness. If I have to be out and about with a semi-wild animal, I want to tramp through long grass – off the beaten track, as those working in the tourism industry would say. After all, a dog is also a creature which is more at home in uncultivated nature, and this is especially true of Winston. Aside from that, I pay dog tax, therefore, it is absolutely Winston's right to tear freshly planted young oak trees out of the soil and chew up the stems as if they were sticks of liquorice. Yes, Winston, do it! Stick your gherkin-nose in the dratted mole hole and dig with your extra-terrestrially giant paws for all you are worth! Haven't you seen the stupid crow? Get it! And when you have exterminated the crow, I'll tip you the wink about the squirrel which is nibbling away, absorbed in building up its winter reserves. One jump and you're there. One bite and you're full.

But of course I don't issue these kinds of commands. Aside from a couple of marginal violations, I observe the rules of decency. But I would still like to know why every morning woodcutters are cutting down the big, old trees ...

THE DOG'S NAME

How do you decide on a name for a dog? Do you give him a typical dog handle like Fifi, Max, Spot or Fido? Or do you baptise him with something that connects him to human society, such as Stephanie, Henry, Emily or Thomas? The name Winston is a gift to a dog like Winston, and I have always wondered how people who thought up such a sophisticated name for their dog could tie that same animal to a tree in the middle of winter and desert him. Or did his previous owners call him Winston because they reckoned he was undiplomatic, belligerent and greedy? Did they perhaps think, "If we call the dog Winston, he'll be strong enough to make it by himself"? Winston Churchill is supposed to have consumed huge amounts of food before he began to put his defence strategy against Hitler into effect. It is, however, a bit hard to believe that people who abandon a dog could be bothered with historical references. Either way, the name Winston was a good choice, otherwise I would have to have called the dog Lex Barker.

There are dog owners who simply can't avoid perpetuating with the choice of name for their

own dog those traits which don't ever improve
through constant imitation: Snoopy, Garfield,
or Beethoven, the latter because of the film
comedy *Beethoven*, which is about a dog. Goofy,
Lassie and Rin Tin Tin, on the other hand,
are hardly ever used any more, as the original
bearers of these names have been forgotten, or
have become so unpopular that no one likes to
remember them. Owners are sometimes very
enamoured of how their dog looks, so a Bull
Terrier owner called his bitch simply Nose, whilst
another – after careful consideration – plumped
for Bully. Diminutive, but no less bandy-legged
dogs answer to the name of Carrot, whilst huge,
hairy animals come when called by the name
Yeti or Shaggy. It is important – according to the
canine specialists whose praises we have already
sung – to give the dog a short name that it will
remember easily.

But what use is it to me if I give my dog a
distinctive name but, when it is called, he just
stands far away wagging its tail, with absolutely
no intention of coming to me? Of course,
Winston understands that he is meant to come
when his name is called and generally this is
what he does. He stops running, looks around
and comes lolloping back happily, like a pet
is supposed to. But then there are also those
moments when the call fades away without
the desired effect; the dog trots through the
long grass and pretends to be deaf. Would he
hear better at that point if his name was Bodo
or Terry? Do dogs get tired of their name at

some stage? During the first few weeks that
he was living with us, I subjected Winston to a
battery of tests, which included the name test.
I called the dog by his name, Winston, and,
as expected, was rewarded with tail-wagging
acknowledgement. Just to be silly, I spoke to
Winston in the same emphatic tones, but called
him Sebastian, and the dog wagged his tail just
as happily. The same thing happened when I
called him variously Lothar, Werner, Else and
Gunther. Nothing matters very much to the dog;
he doesn't even care what his name is, the main
thing is that he is being spoken to, names are
just hollow words and only mean something to
master or mistress.

It's not an infrequent occurrence for dog
names to be inherited by several generations.
When a dog by the name of Macbeth dies, his
owner will keep buying male dogs and calling
them Macbeth. At some point, the first Macbeth
will, however, have been forgotten and then
the second Macbeth, and at some point the
grandchildren will rebel and ask why every dog
has to have the bloody name Macbeth, especially
as nobody knows what Macbeth signifies. So the
next dog is called Gonzo. This dog pride down
the generations is particularly evident in matters
to do with the breeding of pedigree dogs. Dogs
like Carelius von Greiffenstein zu Beerenberg,
who can also produce the associated paperwork
and not just a page ripped out of a Czech
vaccination booklet like Winston. The owners
of these dogs can guarantee the one hundred

per cent purebred nature of their dogs and therefore declare their propagation to be a clean and above-board business, free from surprises. Winston is presumably not a descendant of this kind of family tree. His forefathers must have been Czech lumberjacks, because only this could explain Winston's insistence on dragging huge logs with him all over the place. His purpose in life is work, not labels, as in the case of Carelius von Greiffenstein zu Beerenberg.

The choice of name becomes particularly adventurous if you are going to show your dog professionally. We are talking about the kind of canines that win top prizes at dog shows, either because they are an especially fine example of their breed, or prove themselves capable of exceptional sporting achievements. These kinds of dog are called Little Grise From Friar's Point and Hot Potatoes A Hard Day's Night, or even Little Chilli Peppers Isabel Icepepper – names that bear witness to the great intellectual efforts of their owners and doubtless make a distinguished impression at shows. But what's the point of a name like that at the dog park? How can I call my dog when he's running towards a walker far off in the distance with the sharp command "Come to heel immediately, Brave Paragon's Danterry Diva!"? "Stop chewing the dead mole, Anterrabaee Memorial Indigo!" – does that work? If you rummage about on internet forums to do with dogs, their care, difficulties resulting from their care, etc, you constantly encounter the exhortation to never to buy a dog without papers; he needs to originate from a good family, otherwise problems will occur within a short period of time – so the advice goes. And when the dog does something daft, just hold the papers under his wet nose and say: "Here, Rover, are your papers, which mean that you are officially obliged to be a good, obedient dog. Violations will be punished with expulsion." Or something like that. Winston has no papers; he therefore is and will remain an illegal dog, a quasi-outlaw, even though he wears the City of Munich's official stamp around his neck, which he has meanwhile chewed beyond recognition.

Alien, and yet one of us

Of course, I have become closer to the dog over the last two years. If we look back to those cold winter days when Winston first began to live with us, we tried everything to get rid of him. Despite this, the stealthy poison of affection and familiarity was already at work in us: oh, I know, you hear it time and again from friend and foe – once you have got used to an animal, you can't give it away. But we didn't get used to him! No normal person can get used to an animal that messes up his entire life. Late sleepers become early risers, couch potatoes become athletes, people committed to contemplation become defenders of the joy of barking. In comparison, the dog found settling in much easier; in fact, he probably didn't even have a settling-in phase, unless his habit of biting table legs and chewing carpets were displacement activities that we neglected to have evaluated and consequently controlled by an animal psychologist. "Strange soul!" as Thomas Mann exclaims in his dog idyll. "Such close friends and yet so alien, so

120

different in certain areas that our words are incapable of doing justice to their logic." There is no better way to express the fact that dogs are bewildering.

No one wants to have a permanent gulf of misunderstanding between themselves and something that they deal with on a daily basis, which is why bridges to human society are constructed for dogs all over the place. There are ramps for helping dogs get into cars, fleecy dog beds and cushions, and mobility aids for arthritic dogs. Canine misery is treated with Bach Flower Remedies, dog psychologists help the animals to reattain the equilibrium to which they are entitled, and TV schedules are stuffed with programmes about dog training, dog education, and animal hospitals. There are special training programmes for problem dogs and difficult-to-manage canines. If Germany is ever in danger of becoming extinct through a lack of children, the dogs will certainly see us through. Presumably, the future of this country really does lie with the dog, because why else should there be such a ridiculous number of facilities and tools to enable it to comfortably take up his place at our side?

The assortment of accessories and equipment that we have bought for Winston has been limited in terms of its variety, but over the last two years, have had to buy at least three or four of each item. As the dog grew constantly, the collars got too tight and we had to buy a new one every couple of months – that's just growth and development, and you can't do much about that. But the matter of dog leads was rather different. Every time Winston sat in the back of the car with his leather lead attached to his collar, he regarded the restraining device as an exceptional culinary delicacy, and bit out the choicest parts, which, as everyone knows, are situated just where the snap links are, so that after about a quarter of an hour of his attention, the lead was completely unusable. We had to get a new one, but this was then also partially eaten, and this became a neverending cycle. The dog treats the cute, soft dog beds which we keep having to replace in the same way. At night, he rolls himself up so tightly that he fits exactly in the little round bed and sleeps there quietly until the early morning without any serious incident. During the day, however, he sees the same bed as prey or a tasty meal, taking hold of the cushion in his jaws and shaking it, before really going to work on it with his claws and teeth until the soft, multicoloured filling – the little, fine-grained plastic confetti – is strewn all over the apartment. When this has happened, the dog sees his work as complete, despite the fact that he will have to spend the following night sleeping on the carpet.

As even our dog's basic equipment has such a short half-life, we have had to restrain ourselves from purchasing more expensive, but really more attractive and therefore more essential, accessories, and can only appreciate from afar the things which other people allow their dogs. In Munich city centre, there is a small

shop that sells carefully selected items to lend
a glossy sheen to every dog's life. In the shop
window there is a display of finely crafted dog
collars with sequins inset to depict regal symbols.
If I provided Winston with a collar like this, it
would probably take him about twenty minutes
to chew the silver crown out of the leather and,
depending on what it tasted like, either swallow it
or chew it up. Of course, it is more attractive and
more dignified when a dog can eat out of a bowl
set into a holder made of marble. No reasonable
person can possibly dispute that a dog's life
is better when he spends his nights on a small
four-poster bed with an embroidered canopy
rather than on a soft, Ikea cushion bed. And only
the daybed made of real Indonesian rattan can
guarantee the dog quite the comfort he needs to
enable him to properly get on his master's nerves
again later. There is no dog who would not prefer
the interior decor in his kennel to include marble
vases in the shape of various canine figures.
The canine supplies shop based in Hamburg
– Luxury Dogs – offers chaises longue in three
models: Luxury Dream, Wild Flower and Zebra
Queen, which will provide an enhanced level
of comfort in a city apartment fit for the little
heir to the throne. However, the three sofas are
exclusively designed for dogs. It's hard to say
whether the Alpha flying jacket from the clothing
department at Luxury Dogs is designed for flying
foxes, but after an extensive and exhausting
walk, it's merely a standard convention for an
averagely well-educated dog to don a red lounge

jacket over his coat which has previously been administered to with lavender and peppermint lotion. A dog of the world should always be decently attired before he takes up his position in front of his Exclusive Model Feeding Station, which, standing on four neo-Greek columns, presents a large portion of barbecued ribs for his delectation, followed by some morsels of black pudding biscuits, finishing off with the sweet, but one hundred per cent macrobiotic dessert, DogYog.

Once, my wife brought home a dog's dressing-up costume from a visit to that dog-obsessed country, England. The mythical and historical nature of the costume should have cheered up an open-minded and refined dog – or at least made him curious. Unfortunately, Winston just looked very sad in the green Robin Hood outfit. When we put on his little hat with its jaunty feather, he turned his gherkin-shaped head towards us and looked at us with a mixture of outrage, embarrassment and silent reproach. We immediately liberated him from his undignified get-up and have never dressed him up since.

The dog, in all his savagery and primitive earthiness, obviously presents a problem for the kind of people who feel obliged not just to be civilised, but to dedicate themselves to following a truly refined lifestyle. And perhaps they believe that if they kit out their dog with stylish accessories and provide it with suitable clothing they can tame some of this wildness. Only something like this can explain why so many dogs look like Paris Hilton, or the poodle that, until recently, was often seen strutting through Schwabing because his mistress had had his coat cut so that he looked like a Bavarian lion. But this is all just assumption, as we don't know these people ...

Perhaps this definite turning of humans towards dogs and the desire to let dogs share human luxury goods is in reality evidence of the terrible loneliness endemic in our society. A dog-owning acquaintance of mine insists that this is the case, because, according to him, it is evident that people are hardly able to communicate with each other these days. Communication between human and dog, on the other hand, is very easy; the human says something, the dog does what it is told and everybody is happy. If we allow the dog access to so many areas of human culture, why shouldn't we also open the door to religion for him? The internet store Jewish Bazaar, for example, provides religious dog owners with the opportunity to obtain a handmade kippah (yarmulke) for dogs. A dog who wants to take an active part in Jewish religious celebrations can do this suitably attired with the ornately decorated headwear. A light-hearted way of helping a dog to become acquainted with the active interpretation of the Talmud and its cultural details is to buy him a large, soft toy bone with KOSHER written on the side, and snacks and chewy bones in the shape of the Star of David. A small toy lamb bearing the message

WINSTON ...

BAA MITZVAH completes the religious pet's
set of essential accessories, although anyone
committed to the cheerier end of the spectrum of
religious practice could always add a soft toy pen
with the meaningful BARK MITZVAH version.

No one, as far as I know, is selling
Christening robes and crucifix-shaped snacks for
dogs – yet ...

HAVE WE REALLY DONE EVERYTHING RIGHT?

Winston is now two years old and has failed to live up to some of the hopes we had for him when he reached this age. He has not become any quieter or less energetic, but is still always ready to bring all his strength to bear in involving us in his need for adventure and the great outdoors. He has sharpened my relationship with dogs, inasmuch as I now inevitably have to be aware of their presence. But in spite of that, I'm still reserved when a strange dog approaches me. I stroke the animal's head, because I have to display a certain basic solidarity with his species, but I would never get down on my knees and rub his head the way other dog owners do with Winston. "You will always have a dog now," I was told recently by a woman who had always got new dogs when her old ones died. But I know that's not how it's going to be. There will be no more dogs after Winston. No French ones, no English ones, no American Bulldogs, no Landseers, no Whippets, no Hungarian Sheepdogs. After Winston's demise – which I hope lies far off in the future – it will be very quiet; my late middle age will be characterized by a smug and outrageously laissez faire attitude. I will smile slightly and sympathetically on the odd occasion when I may look across the dog park. And when I hear the masters and mistresses shouting in vain for their Georgies, Tiggers and Spots, who have run off far away into the distance, I will think back with some nostalgia to the times when I returned home from these kinds of expedition, sweaty and covered with mud, tired from intervening in territorial battles and from discussions with other dog owners about the training problems with our animals.

At least, I hope this will be the case; maybe I'll be an eccentric, desperate dog-widower, who stuffs his apartment full of glossy books about Jack Russells, Bull Terriers and Mastiffs and spends hours every day reading them, and sticking huge, coloured dog posters all over his study walls? Will I eventually go completely bonkers and join a club for dog-lovers, or even become a radical animal rights campaigner? I may even be one of those crazy bloggers, who, under a pseudonym like 'Doggyboy' or 'Sweetbuggy,' writes every day bemoaning the extent to which Germany is hostile to dogs.

And yet, Germany is a dog-loving, nay, even dog-crazy nation, but dog owners just don't want to accept this and consider themselves surrounded by enemies everywhere. They don't understand that not all people will fall to their knees with joy when a huge Italian Mastiff is carrying out its olfactory research programme on their hands (or other, more personal places). Of course, there are also hysterical dog-haters, but what species is universally popular? Strangely, the most intolerant people I have met have been dog owners – of the variety that divide the world into politically correct and incorrect dogs.

After two years, my life has been fundamentally restructured, which, I have to admit, I have got a little bit used to. I have a routine whereby I reassure approaching dog owners that my dog will not eat theirs; that my dog jumps up at people, not out of spite, but out of adoration. I can say: he's a male. I can say: yes, he's castrated. And I am brazen enough that when friends tell me about their children, I tell them about Winston, and won't have it that there is any difference between their child and my dog: after all, they are both a constant source of stress. So much for my relationship with Winston and the world. But what about the view from the other side? How does this dog see me, my wife, our apartment and our whole life? There are moments when he stands in the middle of the room on his bandy legs, looking completely bewildered. Sometimes he barks so loudly that people can hear it two streets away. Now and then, he holds his nose up to the wind like an old-fashioned hiker, who is demonstrating that he still knows how to savour the smell of the great outdoors.

Occasionally, he sobs quietly at night. Sometimes, he stares at me for several minutes,

WINSTON ...

as though on the point of working out what unites or divides him and me. But of course his little canine brain can't manage to advance into the world of cognition. In contrast to the master and mistress, who look after him, go to work and take him to dog agility, Winston has no idea that he will die eventually. He will spend the fifteen years that are statistically available to him unencumbered by metaphysical worries. He will run through the world, snuffling, wagging his tail and eating, and he won't give a crap about the glories of Tuscany, Abruzzi and Lake Garda, because Winston would basically prefer crap to any beautiful landscape.

And as for me: I will spend most of these fifteen years at the other end of the lead – and will never know whether all that we have done for Winston has even come close to meeting his expectations.

APPENDICES FOR THE DISCERNING DOG-LOVER

Books for fans of dogs and literature
🐾 *Krambambuli* Marie von Ebner–Eschenbach
Very famous, but really far too sad a story about
the poor dog Krambambuli, who was caught in a
conflict between a hunter and a poacher and, in
the end, starves to death, too ashamed to return
to his master because he has betrayed him.

🐾 *Man and Dog: an Idyll* Thomas Mann
This is probably the most beautiful literary
monument dedicated to the relationship between
humans and dogs. Thomas Mann tells the story
of how Bauschan the Pointer comes from a farm
in Bad Tolz to live with the author's upper-middle
class family, and goes hunting with them in an
amazingly bucolic, but probably mostly fictitious
Munich. One of the most moving scenes in
the story is about a rabbit that is fleeing from
Bauschan. With the fear of death in his eyes, the
prey jumps up at the no-less horrified Thomas
Mann, before he can seek refuge in the green
fields of the Isarauen.

🐾 *Man meets Dog* Konrad Lorenz
The tone of Lorenz's work is initially rather
academic as he describes how the dog has
developed into a pet from its origins as a wolf,
but then writes a very lively account of his life
with various breeds of dog. Some of Lorenz's
training tips do seem a bit brutal today, though,
and have long been superseded by cleverly
devised, non-violent methods.

... the dog who changed my life

🐾 *My little dog Mister* Thomas Winding
A fine children's book about a dog who
introduces himself to the author and explains
that he will be living, eating and sleeping in Mr
Winding's house from now on. And this is what
happens, even though Mr Winding really doesn't
want a dog. Seems somehow familiar ...

🐾 *Hound of the Baskervilles* Arthur Conan Doyle
A complicated case for the ingenious Sherlock
Holmes, which clearly demonstrates the
undesirable effects of giving a dog a phosphorus
compound to eat instead of well-balanced meals.

🐾 *Marley & Me* John Grogan
The story of a married couple who acquire a
fairly lively dog which does some scandalous
things. In the final analysis, however, Marley is
so 'cute' that everybody forgives him and forgets
about all the household items he has ruined.

🐾 *Love on bandy legs* Hans Gruhl
Together with *Marriage on bandy legs*, the
most popular dog story from the 1950s, told
– obviously entirely reliably – from the point of
view of Blasius the dog. Hans Gruhl was also
a popular crime writer and met his end in an
apposite manner: when he wanted to see how
someone could shoot themselves in the head, he
tried it out using a gun with an empty chamber.
    Unfortunately, Gruhl had overlooked the fact
that there was still one bullet in the barrel. He
pulled the trigger and died immediately.

133

🐾 *The Little Encyclopedia for Household Dogs*
Juli Zeh
We have the author's dog, Othello, to thank
for this valuable volume of tips. Othello has
taken the trouble to compile the most important
terms which dogs can use to gain a better
understanding of their master or mistress.
Reference the relevance of the intellectual,
Othello draws attention to the parallel with
the household dog in this respect, as "no one
understands his practical value, but in spite of
this everyone knows that he has to be fed from
time to time." This is, therefore, another book
that is ruthless in demonstrating the closeness
between humans and canines.

🐾 *Four-legged Muses: Authors and their Dogs*
Jurgen Christen
Once again, we can see all the dogs together
with their authors. It's also very nice to read
more about Bella, who was found by Robert
Gernhardt in an Italian car park and saved from
starving to death – the famous photo, which
shows Gernhardt giving Bella a few instructions,
adorns the cover. The record of Bella's rescue
and adoption was written by Gernhardt himself
and you can read it again here in its complete
form. And hats off to Kinky Friedman, who
named his dog Nobody to lend the expression
"Nobody is perfect" a whole new quality.

DOG MANUALS THAT REALLY ARE USEFUL
🐾 *Dog Owner's Manual* Bruce Fogle

British-based Canadian Bruce Fogle is a vet, and one of the most experienced authors of books about dogs around. Furthermore, his offerings are laced with a good dose of British wit, so don't read like lectures.

🐾 *The Other End of the Leash: why we do what we do around dogs* Patricia B McConnell
An unusually unsentimental and realistic book about dogs, which doesn't seek to explain absolutely everything at once, but actually apportions a certain degree of inexplicability to the relationship between human and dog.

🐾 *The world in his head: how dogs learn* Dorothee Schneider:
Dog training practiced in step with the dog's actual capabilities.

FAMOUS PEOPLE AND THEIR DOGS
Frederick II, King of Prussia, always had Greyhounds, and they were almost his only companions in old age. The King oversaw the menu served to the dogs and his flunkies were instructed to only speak to the dogs in French. In so doing, Frederick the Great developed a really elegant method of making people look very unimportant in comparison to dogs.

Wolfgang Amadeus Mozart had a bitch called Pimperl, also known variously as Pimsess, Pimmperl, Miss Pimpes, Bimperl, Bimbel and Pimpes, depending on what mood the genius

was in. That Pimperl was a family dog is proved
by a letter from Mozart's mother containing the
following advice for the maid, Thresel: "... make
sure she keeps busy until I come again and takes
Bimpes out for a piss like a good girl." This kind
of robustly expressed recommendation was
quite in the spirit of the Rococo era, and every
dog owner knows that there are two sides to the
canine being: the requirement-oriented, which
takes us to the dog park in the great outdoors
every day, and the poetic, which enables us
to happily elevate the dog's status to that of
a wondrous being. No one can prove whether
Mozart really later had a dog by the name of
Buzigannerl, but this is suggested by *The artistic
dog (Der kunstreiche Hund)*, a poem of many
verses, that Mozart dedicated to a Buzigannerl:
"Now then, Buzigannerl, the king of all dogs, is
a fruit grown in Vienna, but I do not know the
hour, nor the month, nor the day when Zemir,
his mama, brought him into the world; nothing
is known to us about his gracious papa, neither
status nor name, only that he was an Austrian
noble."

The composer Richard Wagner relied on the
musical instincts of his two dogs when producing
his operas. Peps, for instance, reacted to
Wagner's musical suggestions with empathetic
behaviour. When the master wanted to involve
his dog in the creative concept for the *Ring
of the Nibelungen*, Peps became ill and died.
Wagner got himself another, equally musically

gifted dog called Fips. Whilst out for a walk, Wagner heard how Fips tramped through the bushes and created highly inspired rhythms with his paws. Wagner made a note of Fips' theme and developed it to absolute perfection in his opera *Siegfried*. To be really fair, any mention of Siegfried's journey through the forest should always include the attribution "based on an idea by Fips." In fact, why doesn't every dog owner write an enormous opera? We get to hear rustling bushes and rhythmic scratching every day!

The American author Truman Capote loved to parade amongst the New York upper class and shock them with his Bulldog, Maggie, a fat, ferocious-looking beast. Capote also introduced Maggie to the social scenes in Switzerland, Italy and France. It must be a real pleasure for a refined, cultured, well-educated person with delicate sensibilities to be thwarted by a bullish, bandy-legged dog who doesn't suit him at all.

Sigmund Freud, the inventor of psychoanalysis, warned his patients off stroking his Chow, Yofi, on their first visit, as the dog was unpredictable and prone to snapping. More importantly, Yofi is reputed to have done good analytical groundwork for his master: Yofi would approach peaceful, introverted patients in a relaxed and unreserved manner, though kept his distance from aggressive patients. In addition, Yofi had a very precise internal clock. When a therapy session was due to end, the dog stretched himself and trotted to the door, and the session could finish without Freud having to appear impolite by looking at his watch.

Sometime around 1930, the poet Gottfried Benn, who was not very familiar with the canine world, went on a trip with Gertrud and Paul Hindemith, and their dog Alfi. Maybe Benn was thinking of this outing when he wrote this line in one of his last poems: "Humanity and its moaning is all around you, the married couple and their odious dog"?

A book about Winston can hardly fail to mention his famous namesake. The great British Prime Minister, Winston Churchill, known to his wife as Pug, wrote the following affectionate poem about the poorly little dog, Punch, who belonged to his daughters, Mary and Sarah:

Poor Puggy-wug
Oh, what is the matter with poor Puggy-wug
Pet him and kiss him and give him a hug
Run and fetch him a suitable drug
Wrap him up tenderly all in a rug
That is the way to cure Puggy-wug
(Quoted from Felicitas Noeske: *Das Mopsbuch* (*The Pug Book*))

It's a matter of honour for every American president to bring a dog with him to the Whitehouse. Fala, the Scottish Terrier

owned by Franklin D Roosevelt, was once even
the topic of a political election campaign. The
Republican opposition spread the rumour that,
on a journey around the Aleutian Islands, the
President had forgotten his dog during one of
his transit stops, and had sent a navy destroyer
to pick up Fala, which cost American citizens
several million dollars. In response, Roosevelt
made his famous humorous *Fala Speech*, in
which – to the sound of laughter from his
supporters – he spoke about his dog's outraged
Scottish soul: "He has not been the same dog
since."

Ronald Reagan occasionally let his dog, Lucky,
attend official receptions.

Bill Clinton surprised the Americans when he
moved into the White House with a break in
tradition: instead of a dog, he brought a cat,
Socks, with him. The labrador, Buddy, didn't
move in until four years later. Buddy also made
history – by peeing on the red carpet at Camp
David during the Middle East peace talks.
Barney, George W Bush's Scottie, had his own
website on the official White House homepage,
where you can see the numerous films with
which Barney secured himself a central role in
the seat of government.

The American General George S Patton was
certainly not the most pleasant individual; he
was a fan of brash statements, admired the SS,

WINSTON ...

and was guilty of various other serious offences
against good taste. But he truly loved his white
Bull Terrier, Willie, whose full name was William
the Conqueror, and who followed the General
everywhere, even on the battlefield. When Patton
died in a car accident after the end of the war,
the Bull Terrier lived out the remainder of his
life with Patton's widow. At the Patton Memorial
Museum in Chiriaco Summit in Southern
California, you can see a statue depicting the
General with his white Bull Terrier – there is no
more moving monument to the magical charm of
a human-canine relationship than this sculpture
of the proud, highly-decorated warrior next to his
small, white, bandy-legged Bull Terrier.

The American writer John Steinbeck once felt
that he would have liked to murder his Irish
Setter, Toby. When Steinbeck and his wife were
out, Toby ate half of the only manuscript of the
novel *Of Mice and Men*, which Steinbeck had
just completed. The author said afterwards that
Toby was probably just doing what a critic would
have done. Later, Steinbeck acquired a Poodle,
Charley, whose actual name was Charles le
Chien, and who preferred to be given commands
in French. Steinbeck took Charley with him on
his famous road trip through the USA, which
he then documented in his book *Travels with
Charley*.

George Bush senior's dog, Millie, even had her
biography written – which outsold her master's!

DOGS WHO MADE HISTORY

The first dog in space was called Laika. She was shot into orbit in 1957 with *Sputnik 2* and died of heat exhaustion. Laika was a stray from Moscow, half-Husky, half-terrier, and could have become a shining example of how a poor mutt could rise from the mud to the stars. Sadly, fate showed her no mercy.

Good old Nipper from Bristol had a more comfortable journey to fame. He was another terrier-cross from the streets, but didn't have to endure being catapulted into space in an overheated rocket, just to look into the horn of a gramophone for long periods whilst the artist painted. And Nipper went on to become the famous trademark symbol for various record companies, including EMI in Europe.

The prototype of all search and rescue dogs was doubtless the kindhearted and benevolent Saint Bernard Barry, who saved the lives of more than forty in the early 19th century, one of whom confused poor Barry with a wolf and inflicted serious injuries on him. After this, the prior of the Great Saint Bernard Hospice brought Barry to Berne, where he eventually died, having lived to a very great age. The taxidermists got to work on him and you can see his stuffed remains today in the Museum of Natural History in Berne. And he's **not** wearing a little barrel of brandy.
The idea that a dog models his behaviour on

that of his master is a truism. Thyra, the dog which belonged to Otto von Bismarck, provides excellent proof of this rule: she once brought expression to her master's policy on Russia by biting a large hole in the seat of the trousers of Russian Prime Minister Alexander Gortschakow. Bismarck must have approved, as he felt that Gortschakow was as dangerously vain as Disraeli. It's just as well, then, that the sensitive Benjamin Disraeli never had to visit Bismarck ...

The dog Stuczel could really have been arrested for procurement, because, in the mid-17th century, he spent a great deal of time carrying numerous love letters backwards and forwards between Sir Kurt von Wenckheim and Lady Hilaire von Wangenheim. But because the world is such a sentimental place, the couple, who later married, dedicated a monument to the helpful dog in Winterstein in Thuringia. The inscription is in verse: "Ano 1650 jar, der 19. Marci war, ward ein hund hieher begrawen, das in nicht fressen die Rawen. War sein Name Stuczel genannt, Fursten und Hern wolbekannt. Geschach ub seiner grosse Treuligkeit, die er seine Hern und Frauen beweist." (On 19th March in 1650, we buried a dog here, so that the ravens wouldn't eat him. His name was Stuczel, known to princes and gentlemen. We treasure the great loyalty he displayed to his master and mistress.) In short: he was a good boy, that Stuczel.

142

... the dog who changed my life

DOGS IN FILMS

Dogs have always been popular as film actors, perhaps because of the range of characters that a dog can play – from the exuberant terrier who gets on everyone's nerves, through the loyal friend who rescues people from distress and danger, to the clever police dog which rounds up the criminals with cunning and skill.

The most well-known of the canine film stars was Lassie. However, the first Lassie to appear on film in 1958 was a male dog named Pal; just like the well-known brand of dog food.

Prior to that, the most famous dog on film was the German Shepherd from Lorraine, Rin Tin Tin. Rin Tin Tin was a dog on whom the fates smiled right from the start. An American soldier found him and his mother and two littermates in an abandoned dog kennel, and took him to Los Angeles. He trained the German Shepherd and wrote a film script for him, but couldn't find a producer. Finally, Warner Brothers, which ran a tiny film studio, gave him a chance. Rin Tin Tin's first film, *The Man from Hell's River*, was released in the cinema in 1922 and probably saved Warner Bros from ruin. At any rate, the exceptional dog enabled the Brothers to later produce the box office hits *Casablanca* and *Rebel without a cause*. When Rin Tin Tin died in 1932, he was buried in the pet cemetery in Asnieres-sur-Seine in Paris.

Strongheart, the German Shepherd from

WINSTON ...

Germany, had a film career rather overshadowed by that of Rin Tin Tin. Strongheart was a real German police dog, who even had his own star in the Walk of Fame. Unfortunately, in 1929, he slipped during filming, fell against a spotlight, and died later from his burns. A sad fate: we should probably let dogs be dogs and then they would perhaps not meet this kind of tragic end.

Even before Rin Tin Tin, Pete the pup made his cinematic debut in the children's series *Our Gang*. Petey was an American Pit Bull Terrier (ironic, that this breed is now so reviled). The characteristic, monocle-like circle around his left eye was painted on by the make-up artist.

In more recent times, the film *Beethoven* has done its bit to entertain the dog-loving cinema audience. Beethoven is a Saint Bernard, who is rescued from an evil vet by a nice family. Rescued dog tales are always particularly worth watching, because you expect them to be grateful but not show it to their rescuers, at least not directly.

A more recent canine on film is *Underdog*: "No need to fear, Underdog is here!" The hero is Shoeshine, whose owner is a useless inventor. Shoeshine swallows a particularly strong vitamin preparation by mistake, which gives him the power of flight. Seems like a lot of trouble to go to; in Winston's case, all I have to do it hold up a stick and I swear the dog flies like a rocket.

DOGS ON TV

In the 1970s, Germany's favourite dog was Wum, who was drawn by Loriot and promoted the 'Aktion Sorgenkind' (a charitable organization campaigning for rights for the disabled, now renamed 'Aktion Mensch'), and presented the TV quiz show, *The Big Prize*. His song *Ich wunsch mir ne kleine Miezekatze* (*I want a little pussycat*) was number one in the German charts in 1973.

The American TV detective, Columbo, often blathered on about a dog called Dog, which he owned and for which he had never been able to find a suitable name. Sources say that the dog was supposed to be a Basset Hound.

The dog as independent investigator appears for the first time in the German TV series Inspector Rex, with the title role played initially by the dog Reginald von Ravenhorst, born in Ingolstadt in 1991, and since 2004 by Rhett Butler, born in 1997. The names of the latest 'Rex' stars demonstrate how the owners of these dogs planned their film careers from when the dogs were still puppies.

Most recently, the German Saturday evening series *Here comes Kalle* has introduced another popular canine detective. The title role is played by the Parson Russell Terrier, Brad Pitt vom Mahdenwald, known as Boomer, alternating with the back-up dog, Toby. Of course, one of the police officers doesn't like the dog and thinks his uninhibited antics are inappropriate. But this attitude means that the viewers find him unpleasant and, in short, the message is: everybody loves Kalle and anyone who deviates from the party line is daft and out of step.

Dogs as the subject of educational exercises are particularly popular. The Vox channel has been showing a programme for a few years in which the 'Tiernanny' (animal supernanny), Katja Geb–Mann, explains to despairing dog owners how they can make their wayward pets behave in a socially acceptable manner. But why does the woman always give the dogs Lekkerlis snacks? Doesn't Ms Geb-Mann realise that these things make dogs fat? Fat and stupid.

Some of the worst-behaved dogs in Britain come face-to-face with three tough trainers who hope to tame the difficult animals, *Dog Borstal*, shown on English TV (BBC3).

Cesar Millan's (aka *The Dog Whisperer*) specialty is working with dogs that are known to be aggressive. Episodes of the programme often feature, but are not limited to, work with an aggressive dog, and Millan's application of rules, boundaries, and limitations.

DOGS IN CARTOONS

One of the first cartoons with dogs as the main
characters was Wilhelm Busch's comic strip
about Plisch and Plum, who were rescued by two
boys after the horrible Kaspar Schlich wanted to
drown them in a pond. As was usually the case
in Busch's stories, Schlich later drowns in the
pond himself – as is only fair – and Plisch and
Plum get taken home by an English gentleman.
"May you eat beefsteak every day!" the boys call
after them. Is England really basically paradise
for all dogs?

Snoopy is the contemplative and philosophical
Beagle from the cartoon series *Peanuts*, whose
plan to read Tolstoy's *War and Peace* fails because
he can manage only one word a day, which
makes him the only dog that humans can
identify with.

For decades, the American writer and illustrator
James Thurber provided *The New Yorker*
magazine with drawings in which humans
and dogs experience unusual things because
he allows them to swap roles. In one of his
cartoons, a large dog destroys a woman's hat
that is lying on a chair. When the woman comes
home, the man rips the hat out of the dog's
mouth and chews wildly on it himself, in order
to demonstrate to his furious wife that it was
him and not the well-behaved dog which was
responsible for the vandalism. The fact that

WINSTON ...

The New Yorker still carries on the tradition of dog cartoons today must be viewed as homage to this humorous misanthropist.

In Herge's comic book series, the reporter Tintin's sidekick is the Fox Terrier, Milou. Whilst in Germany the duo operate under the names of Tim and Struppi, which sounds a bit unromantic – Herge had in fact named the clever little dog after his first love, Milou, who was, presumably, grateful that she got to live on in people's hearts as a Fox Terrier.

Idefix first appeared in Gaul in 1963 and offered his services to Asterix the warrior with a decisive 'Woof!' Later, Idefix also joined the warriors in battle and, when necessary, made fiercer sounds, such as 'Grrrrrr!' So – just a normal dog, then.

Pluto, Mickey Mouse's dog, who first appeared in the dog park in 1930, also comes into this category. He's the only creature in the whole of Duckburg who really is an animal and has no human traits whatsoever, although he is once supposed to have said "Kiss me." But perhaps even that is another example of wishful thinking by dog owners who have to anthropomorphize everything pertaining to animals.

Scooby Doo is a detective in dog form, who investigates together with his human friends Shaggy, Daphne, Fred and Velma, though, unfortunately always gets scared very quickly.

148

Slightly surprising, given that he is a Great Dane.

The most famous canine lovers in cartoon history have to be *Lady and the Tramp*. The cocker spaniel and the mongrel have their wildest love scene with the legendary spaghetti kiss. Both of them eat the same pasta strand from either end to meet in the middle with a real film kiss. At the dog park – and I'm just telling you this to free you from any illusions – dogs are more likely to bite each other's flews; then again, I probably shouldn't mention that here.

Dog and master complement each other once again in the cartoon series *Wallace & Gromit*. Wallace is an inventor, but, sadly, most of his experiments go completely wrong. The silent but clever Gromit always saves the day. What dog owner doesn't wish for this kind of companion?

Loriot began his career as an illustrator in the 1950s with dog cartoons for *Stern* magazine, though these were cancelled after only a few appearances because readers found them tasteless. Later, the artist kept Pugs at his country estate beside Lake Starnberg. When he appeared on the ARD chat show *Beckmann*, the 84-year-old Loriot was accompanied by his Pug, Emil.

Muttley, a mixed breed dog, first appeared in *Wacky Races* in 1968, as the sidekick of the nasty but

incompetent and horribly accident-prone villain Dick Dastardly. While Dick was created as the equivalent of Professor Fate from the 1960s movie *The Great Race*, Muttley mirrored the film's character of *Max Meen*. Dastardly and Muttley were paired together in various later Hanna-Barbera series as bumbling villains. Muttley does not really talk; his main examples of speech are his trademark snicker – a wheezing, smoker's laugh (usually made at Dick's expense) – and a mushy, sotto voce grumble against an unsympathetic or harsh Dick (usually along the lines of "Sassafrassarassum Rick Rastardly!")

QUOTES ABOUT DOGS

🐾 *Pick a fight with the dog owners and you will lose the absolute majority!*
Konrad Adenauer

🐾 *Dogs are like people, just with more hair, and they never want any discounts*
Elliot Erwitt (dog photographer)

🐾 *To his dog, every man is Napoleon; hence the constant popularity of dogs*
Aldous Huxley

🐾 *The dog has got more fun out of Man than Man has got out of the dog, for the clearly demonstrable reason that Man is the more laughable of the two animals*
James Thurber

🐾 *Dogs have all the good qualities of people, whilst at the same time having none of their faults*
Frederick the Great

🐾 *A dog reflects the family life. Who ever saw a frisky dog in a gloomy family or a sad dog in a happy one? Snarling people have snarling dogs, dangerous people have dangerous ones*
Arthur Conan Doyle

🐾 *To err is human, to forgive canine*
Unknown

🐾 *Dogs love their friends and bite their enemies, quite unlike people, who are incapable of pure love and always have to mix love and hate*
Sigmund Freud

🐾 *The bond with a true dog is as lasting as the ties of this earth will ever be*
Konrad Lorenz

🐾 *The great pleasure of a dog is that you may make a fool of yourself with him and not only will he not scold you, but he will make a fool of himself too*
Samuel Butler

🐾 *Scratch a dog and you'll find a permanent job*
Franklin P Jones

🐾 *Properly trained, a man can be dog's best friend*
Corey Ford

WINSTON ...

🐾 *A dog is not 'almost human' and I know of no greater insult to the canine race than to describe it as such*
John Holmes

🐾 *The more I see of man, the more I like dogs*
Madame de Stael

🐾 *Near this spot are deposited the remains of one who possessed beauty without vanity, strength without insolence, courage without ferocity, and all the virtues of man, without his vices*
Lord Byron

🐾 *If you get to thinking you're a person of some influence, try ordering somebody else's dog around*
Will Rogers

🐾 *They never talk about themselves but listen to you while you talk about yourself, and keep up an appearance of being interested in the conversation*
Jerome K Jerome

🐾 *A door is what a dog is perpetually on the wrong side of*
Ogden Nash

🐾 *Dogs feel very strongly that they should always go with you in the car, in case the need should arise for them to bark violently at nothing right in your ear*
Dave Barry

🐾 *You're driving along in your car, another car is coming towards you with a dog hanging out the window, mouth open, ears flapping, and you just know he's saying to himself: 'You're a rubbish driver, you're a rubbish driver"*
Lee Evans

🐾 *One reason a dog is such a lovable creature is his tail wags instead of his tongue*
Unknown

🐾 *Outside of a dog, a book is probably man's best friend, and inside of a dog, it's too dark to read*
Groucho marx

FIVE STATEMENTS TO REASSURE ANXIOUS PASSERSBY

🐾 He only wants to play

🐾 He just wants to get to know you better so as to be sure that you don't represent any danger

🐾 He may be a bit too persistent

🐾 He just wants to introduce himself to you quickly

🐾 He won't bite right away

WINSTON ...

WHICH NAMES SUIT WHICH BREED?
Heavy dogs such as Beagles, Bulldogs and
Basset Hounds, answer well to names like Roger,
George or Hercules; slim, hunting types or very
slim dogs like Lurchers and Whippets are called
Ajax, Ashley or Shadow, whilst Rex still suits the
German Shepherd, and Max is always good for a
Dachshund. Dog owners who have absolutely no
idea what to call their dog can find fast, practical
help at www.animalfriends.org.uk/petnames/
www.names-for-dogs.co.uk/ www.i-love-dogs.
com/names/origin/uk_53.html

MISCELLANEOUS
If the human is committed to being politically
correct, then of course the dog must follow suit.
At www.vegandognutritionassociation.com you
will find reasons and guidelines for giving your
dog a meat-free existence.

But it's not just through an environmentally-
friendly diet that our four-legged friends can
work to reduce their carbon paw print as much
as possible; they also need the correct choice
of accessories. Ecologically-sound dogs don't
just sleep on any old dog bed, but have a stylish
designer organic bed from Bella Dogga (www.
belladogga.com), made of organic cotton and
filled with kapok.

And if the ecologically-sound animal – from
time to time and against all expectations – should
sometimes smell unpleasant, this can be dealt

with by using a one hundred per cent safe, non-toxic and eco-friendly spray, 'Pro Biosa.'

Something else that should help salve the dog owner's conscience is the 'JooZoo' mp3 player for dogs – although this is currently only available in Korea. It transmits certain sound waves into the dog's ears, which are designed to have a calming and stress-reducing effect, and will provide consolation to a dog left at home by itself, or calm a nervous hound sufficiently to enable it to travel on a high speed train.

AUTHOR'S NOTE
The photo on the cover is not of Winston, but his representative, as Winston was not available for a photocall due to numerous commitments (apartment renovation activities, gardening work in the English Garden, and eating dog biscuits). Aside from this, as a photo only communicates a small amount of character, Winston would prefer it if his appearance took shape primarily in the reader's imagination after reading about his exploits.

WINSTON ...

'EXCUSE MY DOG' NOTES
(Cut out and use as required)

✂ ....

He didn't concentrate very well in his last training lesson

✂ ....

Sorry, but he doesn't like:
❑ women
❑ men

✂ ....

Sorry, but he is not yet quite able to tell the difference between leather boots and lampposts

✂ ....

Unfortunately, leather gloves are still one of his favourite snacks

✂ ....

I promise our next dog will be a Chihuahua

✂ ....

He can't help it; he doesn't know he is a Rottweiler

✂ ....

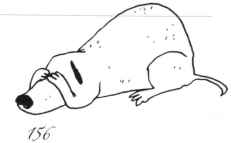

The guide to every aspect of a happy life with
a blind or sight-impaired dog

Hubble & Hattie

MY DOG IS BLIND – BUT LIVES LIFE TO THE FULL!

NICOLE HORSKY

- PAPERBACK • 22x17CM • 80 PAGES
- 20 COLOUR PICTURES, 20 MONO PICTURES
- ISBN: 978-1-845842-91-8
- UPC: 6-36847-04291-2
- £9.99

IT CAN SEEM LIKE THE END OF THE WORLD WHEN THE VET TELLS YOU THAT, SADLY, YOUR BELOVED DOG IS GOING BLIND; IT'S NATURAL TO PUT YOURSELF IN THEIR PLACE AND IMAGINE HOW CATASTROPHIC THIS NEWS WOULD BE …

BUT WITH LIFE-CHANGING EVENTS SUCH AS THESE, THERE'S ONE ESSENTIAL DIFFERENCE BETWEEN THE HUMAN AND CANINE SPECIES: DOGS WON'T WASTE TOO MUCH TIME FEELING SORRY FOR THEMSELVES, OR ASKING "WHY ME?" AFTER TAKING STOCK, THEY WILL – WITH YOUR HELP – ADAPT AND GET ON WITH THE JOYFUL BUSINESS OF LIVING.

THIS INVALUABLE BOOK WILL SYMPATHETICALLY SHOW THE OWNER OF THE NEWLY-BLIND, OR ALREADY BLIND DOG THAT THEIR LOYAL FRIEND IS STILL THE SAME, WITH THE SAME ZEST FOR AND ENJOYMENT OF LIFE. WITH LOVE AND CAREFUL THOUGHT, YOU AND YOUR DOG CAN GET AS MUCH OUT OF LIFE AS YOU ALWAYS HAVE, HAVING FUN AND ESTABLISHING AN EVEN CLOSER BOND AS YOU HELP EACH OTHER FIND NEW OR ADAPTED WAYS TO LIVE TOGETHER

• DIAGNOSIS • EYE PROBLEMS • SOCIALISATION • IN THE HOUSE AND GARDEN • CALMING SIGNALS • STRESS • BASIC COMMANDS • OFF-LEAD • FUN AND GAMES • SMELLORAMA! SCENTING/NOSEWORK • INTEGRATION WITH OTHER DOGS • TRICKS • TIPS FOR TRAINERS • CLOSING THOUGHTS

SMELLORAMA!
NOSE GAMES FOR DOGS

VIVIANE THEBY

- PAPERBACK • 22x17CM • 96 PAGES
- 30 COLOUR PICTURES, 30 MONO DRAWINGS
- ISBN: 978-1-845842-93-2
- UPC: 6-36847-04293-6
- £9.99

WITH UP TO 100 TIMES AS MANY OLFACTORY RECEPTORS AS HUMANS, DOGS USE THEIR SENSE OF SMELL TO 'SEE' AND INTERPRET THEIR WORLD, JUST AS WE DO WITH OUR EYES. A DOG'S KEEN SENSE OF SMELL IS HELPED BY A WET NOSE WHICH HAS A LAYER OF MUCUS THAT ABSORBS SOME SCENT MOLECULES MORE QUICKLY, ALLOWING EVEN THE FAINTEST SCENT TO BE DETECTED AND FOLLOWED.

AND IT'S NOT JUST SPECIALIST HOUNDS SUCH AS GUN, DRUG AND BOMB DETECTION DOGS THAT HAVE THIS AMAZING ABILITY. ALL DOGS LOVE TO SNIFF OUT NEW SMELLS AND MESSAGES – THEIR VERY OWN P-MAIL! – SO YOUR FAITHFUL FRIEND CAN BE TAUGHT TO FIND THOSE LOST CAR KEYS, TELL YOU IF YOUR FOOD CONTAINS MINUTE TRACES OF NUTS, OR EVEN LOCATE A MISSING PERSON, AND IN SUCH A WAY THAT THESE 'NOSE GAMES' ARE GREAT FUN FOR BOTH OF YOU!

- HOW A DOG'S NOSE FUNCTIONS • WHAT YOUR DOG IS TELLING YOU • SCENT DISCRIMINATION
- SIT, STAND, DOWN • HIDE AND SEEK • LAYING A TRACK • CHANGING SCENTS • RETRIEVING • SEARCHING FOR PEOPLE • CITY TRAINING

WAGGY TAILS &
WHEELCHAIRS
– THE COMPLETE
GUIDE TO
HARMONIOUS LIVING
FOR YOU AND YOUR
DOG

ALEXANDER EPP

- PAPERBACK • 22x17CM • 96 PAGES
- 18 COLOUR PICTURES, 9 MONO
  PICTURES
- ISBN: 978-1-845842-92-5
- UPC: 6-36847-04292-9
- £12.99

WAGGY TAILS &
WHEELCHAIRS

The complete guide
to harmonious
living for you and
your dog

Alexander Epp

Hubble & Hattie

CONFINED TO A WHEELCHAIR OR
MOBILITY SCOOTER BUT STILL WANT A DOG – IS THAT A GOOD IDEA?

YES! AS THE AUTHOR – WHO'S WHEELCHAIR DEPENDANT – ABLY DEMONSTRATES. HERE,
EVERYTHING THAT MOBILITY-IMPAIRED POTENTIAL DOG OWNERS NEED TO CONSIDER TO ENABLE THEM TO
OWN AND CARE FOR THEIR VERY OWN CANINE COMPANION IS DESCRIBED AND ILLUSTRATED IN DETAIL.

WHEELCHAIR AND MOBILITY SCOOTER USERS FACE THEIR OWN PARTICULAR CHALLENGES WHEN IT
COMES TO DOG OWNERSHIP: HOW WILL THEY WALK THEIR DOG; TRAIN AND TEACH IT; PLAY GAMES WITH
IT, AND, ALL IMPORTANTLY, PICK UP THAT POOP?

FROM HIS UNIQUE VIEWPOINT, THE AUTHOR ANSWERS ALL OF THESE QUESTIONS AND CONCERNS,
AND MORE BESIDES, ALLOWING READERS TO ASSESS AND DETERMINE WHETHER THEY CAN SHARE
THEIR SPECIAL LIFESTYLE WITH A DOG, AND WHAT THEY CAN DO IN PREPARATION OF THIS HAPPY
CIRCUMSTANCE.

- BENEFITS OF DOG OWNERSHIP • POSITIVE EFFECTS ON STATE OF MIND • BASIC CONSIDERATIONS
- PHYSICAL RESTRICTIONS • CARING FOR YOUR DOG • WALKIN' THE DOG • CLOTHING • SPECIAL
  EQUIPMENT • SUITABLE BREEDS • DOG SIZE AND TEMPERAMENT • ABILITY/SELECTION/ACQUISITION
- TRAINING FOR A SPECIAL LIFE • WALKING BEHAVIOUR • NIGHT-TIME EXCURSIONS • WINTER-TIME
- THE LAW, YOU AND YOUR DOG • ON TOUR • WHEELCHAIR, DOG AND COMPETITION • WATER
  SPORT • YOUR DOG AND TRAVELLING • IDEAS FOR TRIPS • WHEELCHAIR, YOUR DOG AND TRAFFIC •
  GENERAL PROBLEMS • WHERE NEXT? • APPENDIX

160